MINNESOTA
1858

WISCONSIN
1848

MICHIGAN
1837

MAINE
1820

VT.
1791

N. H.
1788

NEW YORK
1788

MASS.
1788

CONN.
1788

R. I.
1790

IOWA
1846

ILLINOIS
1818

INDIANA
1816

OHIO
1803

PENNSYLVANIA
1787

N. J.
1787

MD.
1788

DEL.
1787

MISSOURI
1821

KENTUCKY
1792

WEST
VIRGINIA
1863

VIRGINIA
1788

MA

907

ARKANSAS
1836

TENNESSEE
1796

NORTH CAROLINA
1789

SOUTH
CAROLINA
1788

MISS.
1817

ALABAMA
1819

GEORGIA
1788

LOUISIANA
1812

FLORIDA
1845

DATES OF ADMISSION
of the Forty-eight States

The Growth of a Nation

"Across the Continent"

In 1729 the genial British Bishop of Cloyne wrote some "Verses on the Prospect of Planting Arts and Learning in America," in which he forecast the development of "Time's Noblest Offspring." The last stanza of his poem began "Westward the course of empire takes its way." This line was seized upon by enthusiastic Yankees to dramatize their hopes and aspirations for westward expansion—their "Manifest Destiny."

Photo: Currier and Ives print from Library of Congress

The Growth of a Nation

A Pictorial Review of the United States of America

From Colonial Days to the Present

By EMERSON M. BROOKS

Introduction by Henry Bamford Parkes, Ph.D.

Professor of American History, New York University

E. P. Dutton & Co., Inc., New York

1956

TO

HELEN AND MARSHALL

❧

Library of Congress Catalog Card Number 56–5258

LITHOGRAPHED BY THE MURRAY PRINTING COMPANY

CONTENTS

MAPS

ACKNOWLEDGMENTS

Because this book includes material accumulated over a long period, it is impossible to give due credit to all who have contributed. High on the list are photographers (some now unknown) who captured an instant of history for reproduction here. Alongside them would be those ever-helpful custodians of picture files in numerous museums, libraries, archives, art galleries, chambers of commerce, historical societies, trade associations, and private concerns throughout the country. The author is especially grateful to Miss Virginia Daiker, Carl Stange, and Donald Holmes of the Library of Congress; Miss Josephine Cobb and her associates at the National Archives; Craddock Goins, Edward C. Kendall, C. Malcolm Watkins, Herbert W. Kreiger, John C. Ewers, Miss Margaret Brown, Mendel Peterson, and Frank T. Taylor of the Smithsonian Institution.

Our thanks also to: C. A. Anderson, Presbyterian Historical Society, Philadelphia; Charles A. Anderson, U.S. Geological Surveys; Bryant Baker, Gainsborough Studios, New York; Jerrold M. Ballinger, American Trucking Association; A. K. Baraginvanath, Museum of the City of New York; Mrs. G. Philip Bauer, Carnegie Institution of Washington, D.C.; Mr. and Mrs. Merritt Beeson, Beeson Museum, Dodge City, Kansas; Miss Myrtle D. Berry, Nebraska State Historical Society; H. E. Boing, Jr., Detroit Convention and Tourist Bureau; William R. Breyer, American National Red Cross, Washington, D.C.; Walter J. Brown, San Francisco, California; W. C. Burk, Atchison, Topeka and Santa Fe Railway System, Topeka, Kansas; E. Milby Burton, Charleston, South Carolina, Museum; Harold L. Byrd, U.S. Bureau of Reclamation; Paul H. Cassidy, Field Enterprises, Inc.; Robert Chesnut, Auburn, Alabama; Dr. Harry C. Chubb, Hershey, Pennsylvania; Mrs. Marilyn A. Claire, Corcoran Gallery of Art; Miss Elizabeth Clare, M. Knoedler and Company, Inc.; W. M. Coffman, Islam Temple, San Francisco, California; Mrs. C. E. Cook, Oklahoma Historical Society; W. A. Coons, Union Pacific Railroad; John Cummings, Bucks County, Pennsylvania, Historical Society; Fred T. Darville, Bellingham, Washington; Richard K. Degenhardt, St. Augustine, Florida; J. Huber Denn, Delaware State Chamber of Commerce; Walter C. Densmore, Mount Vernon, Virginia, Ladies Association; Howard J. Douglass, Middlesborough, Kentucky; Leon DeBalinger, Jr., Delaware Public Archives Commission; Harold E. Edgerton, Massachusetts Institute of Technology; C. B. Egolf, Somerset, Pennsylvania; Louis Fanget, U.S. Information Agency; Miss Clare E. Follette, Vermont Historical Society; Miss Elizabeth B. Foran, University of South Carolina; James T. Forrest, State Historical Society of Colorado; Elmer L. Franker, Okahoma Historical Society; General W. H. Frank, Sears Roebuck & Co.; H. L. Fried, Louisville, Kentucky; R. D. Gage, III, Port Gibson, Mississippi; Mrs. Jean L. Geyer, Wyoming Commerce and Industry Commission; David Glick, Henry Ford Museum and Greenfield Village; L. W. Goldberg, J. R. Watkins Company; John Golden, Plymouth, Massachusetts, Chamber of Commerce; J. William Graham, Alabama State Chamber of Commerce; Miss Margaret Hackett, Library of the Boston Athenseum; C. D. Hall, Sutter's Fort State Historical Monument; C. M. Hall, The National Grange, Springfield, Massachusetts; Reba E.

Hammond, Birmingham, Alabama; Miss Shirley Harden, Selznick Studio; Bayless E. Hardin, Kentucky Historical Society; Mrs. George L. Harrison, Stratford Hall, Virginia; L. F. Hart, Gloucester, Massachusetts; Miss Margaret Harvey, Daniels and Fisher Stores Co., Denver, Colorado; Charles E. Hatch, Jr., Yorktown, Virginia, Colonial National Historical Park; Mrs. Lilla M. Hawes, Georgia Historical Society; Thomas K. Hodges, Pennsylvania Public Relations, Harrisburg; Miss Lola M. Homsher, Wyoming State Archives and Historical Department; Leo L. Jacobs, Charles T. Branford Co., Boston; Walter Jacoby, Connecticut State Department of Education; Miss Julia Jarvis, The Champlain Society, Toronto, Canada; Romana Javitz, New York City Public Library; Miss Peggy Kerr, Salt Lake City, Utah; Miss Clare Kessell, Iowa Development Commission; Miss Pricilla Knuth, Oregon Historical Society; Dean F. Krakel, University of Wyoming; Francis Lackey, University of Virginia; Miss Mary R. Mackey, Pioneer Village, Salem, Massachusetts; Arnold L. Magnuson, Beatrice, Nebraska; Alex L. Martin, American Automobile Association, Washington, D.C.; Mrs. Ann L. Marvin, Norfolk, Virginia, Chamber of Commerce; Miss Illa J. Mason, Columbia, Tennessee; Philip P. Mason, Michigan Historical Commission; Miss Grace H. Mayer, Museum of the City of New York; C. B. Mayshark, East Hampton, New York; C. Boone McClure, Panhandle-Plains Historical Museum, Canyon, Texas; Miss Helen M. McFarland, Kansas State Historical Society; Miss Anne Hinkel Miller, Bucks County, Pennsylvania, Historical Society; B. Montgomery, Montgomery Foto Service, Kansas City, Mo.; Paul Moore, Tennessee Department of Conservation; Miss Helen I. Morris, U.S. Vanadium Co., New York; Hugh Morton, Wilmington, N.C.; Gordon Munson, Iowa State College; William Forsythe, Henry Herrell, Albert Matthews, Wayne Rasmussen, and Robert Turnure, Department of Agriculture; Harold Peterson, Department of the Interior; O. L. Mims, Foreign Operations Administration; T. D. O'Hearn, Cadillac Motor Car Division, Detroit; Allan R. Ottley, California State Library; Miss Marguerite Owen, Tennessee Valley Authority, Washington, D.C.; Charles Parker, North Carolina Department of Conservation and Development; Mrs. Gertrude Morton Parsley, Tennessee State Library and Archives; Robert L. Parsons, Associated American Artists Galleries, New York; Philip Pearls, American Federation of Labor, Washington, D.C.; E. A. Phillips, Montana Stockgrowers Association, Helena; Earl W. Porter, Duke University; Stephen T. Riley, Massachusetts Historical Society; F. T. Russell, Hannibal, Missouri; H. L. Schall, Ponca City, Oklahoma; William E. Schupp, Frankfort, Kentucky; Floyd C. Shoemaker, Historical Society of Missouri; Benjamin E. Shore, Cairo, Illinois; Miss Irene Simpson, Wells Fargo Bank History Room, San Francisco; Thomas J. Sinclair, Association of American Railroads, Washington, D.C.; Miss Priscilla Staples, The Wayside Inn, South Sudbury, Massachusetts; J. George Stewart, Architect of the Capitol; William A. Stewart, Atlanta, Georgia; Mrs. Kenneth G. Stowell, New Hampton, New York; Edwin H. Spencer, American Trucking, Inc., Washington, D.C.; George Sykes, U.S. Vanadium Company, New York; N. C. Tanselle, Caulfield and Shook, Louisville, Kentucky; J. F. Townsend, Vermont Marble Company, Proctor, Vermont; William H. Tripp, Old Dartmouth Historical Society and Whaling Museum, New Bedford, Massachusetts; Miss Irene Tucker, New Hampshire State Planning and Development Board; Leslie H. Unger, Rutgers University; Edward J. Urban, Pennsylvania Turnpike Commission, Harrisburg; Ernest Van Harlingen, E. B. Crocker Art Gallery; Miss Virginia Walton, Historical Society of Montana; D. W. Watkins, Clemson Agricultural College; Captain Frederick Way, Jr., Sewickley, Pennsylvania; Ralph J. Weil, The Art Institute of Chicago; Glover Wilkins, Jr., Columbus, Mississippi; Herman W. Williams, Jr., Corcoran Gallery of Art, Washington, D.C.; Ted R. Worley, Arkansas Department of Archives and History; Dr. Harry Wyman, State Department; W. E. Younger, Library of Congress; and Carma R. Zimmerman, California State Library.

For arousing my latent interest in history, grateful acknowledgment is made to Professors Bernard Schmidt and Earle D. Ross, and the late Colonel Rumsy Campbell; for stimulating and sustaining that interest over the years a deep bow to the authors of many books, articles, and scholarly papers, a few of which are recorded in the bibliography. For prolonged, careful, and pleasant assistance, none exceeds that of Miss Lillan Breshears who, among numerous other chores, typed the manuscript.

E. M. B.

INTRODUCTION

Historians have traditionally been concerned mainly with the activities of kings, generals and statesmen. But American history must be written in a different way. In order to understand the growth of the United States, it is necessary to concentrate on the ways of living, achievements and aspirations of average citizens. The United States has produced great men, but her development has been due primarily not to the leadership of outstanding figures or to the authority of the government but to the spontaneous enterprise and energy of countless obscure individuals. While the American record has by no means been devoid of errors and misdeeds, it has demonstrated, on the whole, the capacity of the average man to make constructive use of political freedom and to respect the rights of others.

The United States is a vast and complex country, but the essence of its story can be summarized in a few simple sentences.

In the seventeenth century men and women from different European countries began to cross the Atlantic in order to make new homes for themselves in what was then an unexplored wilderness. This was the beginning of a long process of migration which brought to the United States a series of ethnic groups from almost all other parts of the world and which, in spite of legal limitations, still continues today. Thus the United States has become a new kind of nation, a nation whose citizens are bound together not by common ancestry and traditions but by common ideals and hopes for the future.

Having established themselves along the Atlantic coastline, the Americans of the eighteenth century won their independence from European control and proclaimed the revolutionary doctrine of the equality of man. They went on to create a new kind of federal government, based on the principle of combining the unity of the whole with individual freedom and regional diversity. During the following century they settled the whole immense territory between the Atlantic and the Pacific and built an industrial system based on machine technology and mass production. Meanwhile, the cultural inheritance which they had brought from Europe was slowly modified in the American environment, and they began to evolve new ways of thinking and new art forms expressive of the new American spirit. Finally, having grown in only three centuries from a few struggling colonies to a world power, they began to assume some of the responsibilities of leadership in Western civilization.

This book presents the basic facts of American development in a new way. It tells the story of the American people as a whole, not merely of their political history but of their characteristic activities and ways of living in all sections of the country. It shows what kinds of men and women came to the New World, the places where they settled and the tasks and problems which they faced and mastered, and their progress toward the control of natural forces and toward political and cultural maturity.

The Growth of a Nation concludes by depicting the United States of today, a country whose institutions are still based on the ideals of freedom and equality and which has discovered how to combine national unity with an astonishing variety of ethnic, cultural and regional differences. Interpreted in this manner, the American story has a richness, color and human significance which will surprise those who know it only through more conventional political narratives.

Henry Bamford Parkes

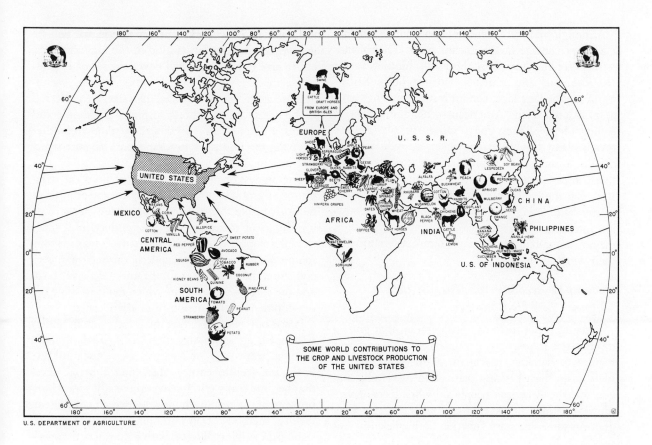

I. AUTHOR'S FOREWORD

A trip around the United States of America is interesting, instructive and thought-provoking. This statement is true whether the traveler is a visitor from abroad or a native son seeing more of his country than the community in which he was born and has grown up. Because of its size and diversity, seeing America, if that term may be used as a synonym for the U.S.A., resembles the six blind men "seeing" an elephant. Every section has something in common with other parts of the country, but distinctive features or ways of life or habits of thought prevent generalizations and sweeping conclusions. A traveler needs a seeing eye and understanding heart to properly interpret the varying scenes and shifting mores encountered along his way.

It's a Big Country, but Others Are Larger

Perhaps the first thing that impresses a traveler is the size of the country. It extends 3,000 miles from East to West and 1,500 miles from North to South, an area of about three million square miles. Even so, Brazil, Canada, China, and Russia are larger, and Australia is only slightly smaller. Russia proper is more than twice the size of the U.S.A.; the whole USSR is nearly three times larger.

The population of the United States is only a third that of China, half that of India, and forty million less than that of the USSR. Compared to the world's population of more than 2½ billion, that of the U.S.A. is small indeed.

Someone has remarked that the "average" American does not know where his forebears came from and cares less. In other words, the American people are a mixture of many nationalities; with some exceptions, they have little interest in tracing their ancestry back to Europe or elsewhere or in maintaining a clear, unadulterated strain. Americans usually accept the principle that cross-fertilization of ideas, customs, and people is more desirable than narrower concepts of isolation and restriction.

Although no exact determination can be made, a high percentage of Americans have a British ancestry. Yet no American thinks of himself as an "Englishman," and principal evidences of the British strain are the language, certain institutions that have been adapted to the American scene, and a general feeling of friendliness for a valiant people. As one travels about the U.S.A., however, he will discover certain areas where people are predominantly of Swedish or German or French or Spanish extraction. But even these distinctions are rapidly disappearing as the assimilating processes of travel, military service, intermarriage, radio, television, motion pictures, magazines, public schools, and community efforts do their work.

Geography Accounts for Much of the "Bigness" in This Country

Distance is not the only consideration that gives a traveler the impression of bigness. Skyscrapers and mammoth factories, machines, grain elevators, railroad yards, meat packing plants and steel mills suggest that the American people are worshipers of size. However, these items exist primarily because they perform some necessary function both efficiently and economically. Because necessity is truly the "mother of invention," these conspicuously big things have been created to meet pressing needs and solve difficult problems.

The vastness of this country caused inventors to create improved and rapid transportation facilities capable of hauling tremendous loads over long distances and to develop rapid communication systems. Because of a relatively small labor force, much attention has been given to labor-saving devices, mechanization, and such processes as assembly-line production to increase output per worker.

In many aspects of American life a penchant for the big and impressive is not noticeable. For example, the average American home is relatively modest and unpretentious, with emphasis on practical usefulness and efficient operation. Even among the wealthy, only a few people reveal a desire for impressive estates. The executive mansion of the President (The White House) is essentially the displaced country home of a well-to-do gentleman and is humble compared to the castles, palaces, and sumptuous estates available to the heads of many other governments. The Capitol Building in which the Senate and House of Representatives carry on the affairs of the nation is an enlarged county courthouse. The Cathedral of St. John the Divine in New York, when completed, will be the largest structure of its kind in the United States, but in size it will rank well down the list of impressive cathedrals of the world. Simplicity and usefulness are more highly regarded than size, are preferred to the ornate. Most Americans prefer the simple and dignified lines of the Tomb of the Unknown Soldier in Arlington Cemetery to some more elaborate structure as a memorial to sacrifice and valor.

The bigness of things in America reflects the magnitude of problems encountered and is the product of necessity rather than a worship of bigness, *per se*. The big things of today are the end products of a long, slow developmental process. Actually, it was the one-room school, the one-room church, the one-room general store, the one-lane road, the one-stack river boat, and the single-track rail line which made possible the development of this nation from a wilderness.

It was only yesterday that the U.S.A. was an underdeveloped, agricultural nation using methods little changed from those of ancient times. Not until late in the nineteenth century when the Industrial Revolution became really effective was there any general improvement in farm machinery, household equipment, factory methods, transportation, and the general standard of living. Today, with accumulated knowledge, increased skills, improved communication and willingness to learn and to adopt new ideas, techniques and procedures, great advances and improvements can be rapidly achieved.

The U.S.A. Is a Product of all Nations

To a large extent, the U.S.A. was developed on borrowed money, on borrowed ideas, crops, livestock, cultures and "know-how." Immigrants brought tools and equipment customarily used in their home countries and plants, seeds and livestock which they diligently propagated. Ship captains, diplomats, missionaries and others traveling abroad from this new country were to bring or send back seeds, plants and useful ideas. Thus a multitude of crops, livestock and new ways of doing things were tried out; those that prospered became a part of the American mosaic. The accompanying map indicates sources of a few of these gifts and a little of what the U.S.A. owes foreign lands.

It is true that some plants native to America became important in the economy and diets of Europe and elsewhere. Corn, or maize, which was unknown abroad prior to Columbus, is now the most widely produced crop in the world. Tobacco at first was erroneously considered of great medicinal value, but later the "divine weed" became widely popular for the pleasure it provided. The potato got off to a bad start in Europe where it was considered so injurious to health that a "Society for Prevention of Unhealthful Diets" was organized against it. (The society's initials "SPUD" became a nickname for the potato, now a major food item to millions of people throughout the world.) America has carried on a healthy interchange with many other countries and is still doing so.

We Lived Longer as Colonies than as States

Like so many other countries, the U.S.A. has had a long and eventful colonial history. In fact, the people of the U.S. should be experts in colonialism since they have had experience under the Spanish, French, English, Swedes, Dutch and Russians. The areas involved and periods of duration varied, but large parts of the U.S.A. were under colonial rule longer than they have existed as states. Florida, for example, was a colony from 1565 until 1819 when it became a part of the U.S.A.; it attained statehood in 1845. Thus Florida was a colony for 254 years and not until the year 2099 will it have been a state for as long as it was a colony.

Our colonial background provides a bridge of understanding, uniting us with colonial and former colonial people everywhere. We learned much from our colonial overlords, however, and we bear them no ill will. From the English we learned the tenets of government; from the French, respect for the law; from the Spanish, a love of color (what a drab land this would be without it). The Swedes taught us cooperation and the Dutch, commerce. These illustrations could be multiplied.

All Americans Are Immigrants

There has never been any clear-cut claimant to the land making up the U.S.A. Columbus was an Italian sailing for Spain; Cabot was an Italian in the service of England; Hudson was an Englishman employed by the Dutch; Cabrillo was a Portuguese working for Spain; Amerigo Vespucci was an Italian commissioned by Portugal. Parts of the U.S. have been held by a succession of foreign powers. New Orleans, for example, has flown flags of three nations. In view of conflicting claims, it seems proper that no single nation was the victor. Instead this country has become in actual fact a land of freedom for all races, colors and creeds.

The purpose of this book is to review the dramatic story of how these divergent elements learned to live together and to develop states united at long last from self-centered, isolated, individualistic, and culturally different colonies.

Looking Eastward to the Sea

A good place to get oriented and to think about this country, its past and future and its various regions, is at the top of the Washington Monument, 555 feet above the earth where windows look to the East, South, North, and West.

To the East lies the velvety green Mall leading toward the Capitol Building, topped by the Goddess of Freedom. Far beyond are sandy coastal plains leading to the broad Atlantic Ocean. The Capitol Building is the center of the great experiment in self-government to which this nation is dedicated and which is a dream of peoples throughout the world.

Photo: USDA by Ware

Away to the South

The window to the south looks out over the Jefferson Memorial and the Potomac River, past the National Airport toward Tobaccoland, the Cotton Kingdom, Florida's sunshine, the bayous of Louisiana, and the rich pine forests of Arkansas.

Photo: USDA by Ware

North toward Canada

From the north window can be seen the baseball fields on the Ellipse, the White House and famous Sixteenth Street. This broad avenue leads past foreign embassies, the pleasant fields of Maryland, and to the industrial North, with its busy multitudes, farms, and factories bursting with activity and supplies for all the world.

Photo: USDA by Ware

West to the Pacific

To the west, beyond the reflecting pool and the Lincoln Memorial, the Potomac River and the rolling hills of the Piedmont, are the Alleghenies and the Mississippi Valley. There the West begins with the Great Plains rising steadily to the Rocky Mountains, and, beyond them, the glamorous coast and the wide blue Pacific. Take another look to the west, where the story of America unfolds. Since the first adventurous settlers moved up the James River, or out of the "crowded" Massachusetts Colony to the fertile valley of the Connecticut River, more than three hundred years ago, Americans have been "going West," and it was largely the life and psychology of the ever-shifting frontier that made us the nation we are today.

Photo: USDA by Ware

Lay of the Land

Along the Atlantic Coast is a low sandy plain, narrow in Maine and widening toward the South, lined with slow-moving rivers gliding eastward to the sea. To the west rises the Appalachian Mountain Range, extending from Maine to Alabama, and known sectionally as the Adirondack, Catskills, Allegheny, Blue Ridge, and Great Smokies. These mountains were the first in the United States to thrust their heads above the flood waters in the distant past before the Ice Age. At one time they were higher than the current highest peak, Mt. Mitchell, North Carolina, of 6,684 feet.

Beyond these rugged and tree-covered mountains lies a vast middle valley formed by the Great Mississippi River in the center, with the Ohio River as its eastern arm, and the muddy Missouri River stretching off to the West with countless smaller tributaries. Beyond the central lowlands rising gently a thousand miles to the West lie the flat, treeless, semiarid Great Plains. Next are the vast Rocky Mountains which form a segment of the 10,000 mile chain of rugged mountains reaching from Alaska through Canada, the United States, Central America and along the western portion of South America. In the U.S.A. they

encompass an immense area more than a thousand miles wide and ranging from border to border. They are interspersed with long fingers of craggy mountains and numerous valleys, huge dry basins, high plateaus, innumerable snow-capped peaks, and occasional winding, twisting rivers. Mount Whitney, 14,495 feet, is the highest peak, but others are nearly as high and all are forest-covered up to timberline, where biting temperatures cut off growth.

The Pacific Coast is a region of many contrasts with Death Valley, 280 feet below sea level and the lowest point in the United States, lying at the foot of Mt. Whitney. All along the coast from Canada to Mexico rambles an intermittent range of low mountains and barren hills which form the western borders of inland valleys.

A cross section of the United States from east to west represents a series of ups and downs. First a gentle incline from the Atlantic Ocean to the moderately high Appalachian Mountains; then down a long bumpy way to the Mississippi River and up again gradually and almost imperceptibly a thousand miles or more to the towering Rockies; then down again in irregular fashion to the beaches of the Pacific Ocean.

II. IN THE LONG AGO

NOMADS FROM ASIA WANDER ONTO A NEW CON-
TINENT—REGIONAL GROUPS OF INDIANS DE-
VELOP—NORSEMEN MAKE A FLEETING VISIT—
COLUMBUS DISCOVERS A NEW WORLD—CABOT
CRUISES ATLANTIC COAST OF NORTH AMERICA

Throughout many millions of years the area now known as the U.S.A. enjoyed a tropical climate. Dinosaurs and other warm weather monsters roamed at will. Then came the Ice Age when thick sheets of ice flowed over the northern part of the country. The ebb and flow of the glaciers as they advanced and retreated, over periods of thousands of years, leveled some land, piled up rock in other spots, gouged out giant holes which became tremendous lakes, and drained the ocean into some areas and then shoved it out again. The last retreat was about 20,000 years ago. According to some scientists, we are now enjoying an interlude between ice ages and, in due course, glaciers will return.

When the ice sheets last receded, the surface of the United States apparently looked much like it does today. Into this wilderness wandered people from Asia whom we know as Indians. After several thousand years some Vikings touched the northeast coast. Finally, after a few more hundred years, Columbus made his famous voyage, followed shortly afterward by Cabot. The solitude of a slumbering continent was ended.

THE AMERICAN INDIANS' PATH TO THE NEW WORLD

During the Ice Age thousands of years ago, a strip of land between Asia and North America formed a bridge over which certain peoples of Asia found their way into Alaska. These travelers—perhaps hunters following game—moved south around the ice sheets. Some went as far as Central and South America. They took on new languages and customs, and formed separate tribes. These peoples of Asiatic origin were named "Indians" by the Spanish discoverers of the New World.

Wanderers from Asia

The story of people in the area now known as the United States of America begins in the dim past with certain nomadic huntsmen about which little is known. Lacking definite knowledge, scientists have developed the theory that at one time Alaska and Siberia were joined, thus forming a land bridge over which natives of Asia wandered onto a new continent some fifteen thousand years ago. These first arrivals presumedly were the foundation stock of the American "Indian." Generally the Indian of the western hemisphere is not thought of as an agriculturist, but the fact is that he learned to produce and use a number of crops such as tobacco, beans, and, most important of all, corn, which he developed from a wild plant not known today. This itself was no mean accomplishment; in fact, it has been called the greatest "plant-breeding job in all history."

The trail of the Indian was lost through centuries of wandering up, down, and across the continent in search of survival, and when the Europeans arrived the Indian no longer knew where he had come from.

Photo: Courtesy of the Chicago Natural History Museum

Principal Types of Indians

In the great forest stretching from the Atlantic Ocean to the Mississippi River lived tribes of Indians in roughly defined areas of influence.

Canoes made of birch bark or from the trunks of trees provided swift and easy transportation on thousands of rivers and streams. Wild animals, including buffalo and elk, roamed the woodlands; ducks and geese filled the air, making the area a hunter's paradise. Beyond the forests lay the Great Plains, at that time probably containing few Indians. In the south-west, village dwellers built their homes of clay and carried on a precarious agriculture. In the Rocky Mountain area and along the California coast, seed gatherers struggled for existence. In the northwest, fishermen speared salmon in the Columbia River and enjoyed fishing in the beautiful rivers formed by the melting snows of the Cascade Range.

Photo: Courtesy of the Chicago Natural History Museum

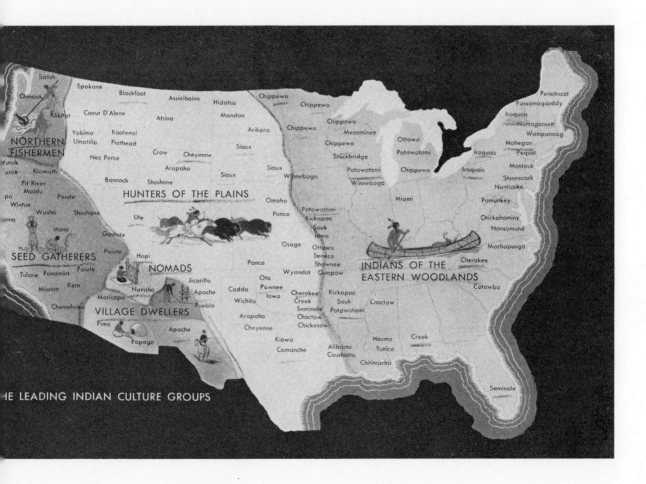

THE LEADING INDIAN CULTURE GROUPS

Combat Between the Ojibwas and the Sacs and Foxes on Lake Superior

North American Indians fought furiously among themselves for as far back as anyone could remember. This internecine strife, combined with losses from smallpox and other illness and plagues, retarded growth of the Indian population. No census was ever taken, but informed guesses are that the Indian population of the entire area within the present boundaries of the United States was probably around 850,-000 people in the days of Columbus. Of this number, perhaps a hundred thousand lived in the area east of the mountains from Maine to Florida. Thus when the Europeans arrived, they were confronted with a thin sprinkling of Indians scattered over an immense area, armed with archaic weapons and bitterly divided among themselves. During the 250 years when the white man was extending his control over the continent, Indians continued to fight among themselves. It is estimated that more Indians were killed by brother redskins than by "palefaces" from beyond the sea.

Conflict between the ways of life of the Indians and homemaking settlers was inevitable and could not be resolved until one or the other gave up the struggle. The plow was the Indian's mortal enemy; it forced destruction of the forests so that crops might grow. With the forests went the wild game upon which the Indian depended for food, clothing, and shelter. The North American Indian was quick to see his situation. By nature a fighter and having no intention of giving up the ways of his ancestors, he fought back as best he could, bravely and with honor. It was, of course, a losing battle against superior numbers and superior equipment, but most of all against a way of life which left the Indian no chance to compromise. He either had to give way before it, accept it, or die.

Photo: Library of Congress

Buffalo Hunt Without Horses

In the centuries before Columbus, with neither horses nor guns, the Indians living in buffalo country had great difficulty in killing these rugged, thick-skinned animals. Occasionally an exhausted buffalo was discovered floundering in the snow and became an easy prey to the Indians, but the most effective method of obtaining buffalo meat, although a very wasteful one, was to frighten a herd into stampeding over a cliff where they were killed or so badly crippled that men on foot could dispose of them. This procedure involved secreting Indians with blankets at regular intervals along the edges of a pie-shaped wedge leading from the precipice, and placing a fleet runner disguised in a buffalo robe in the center of the triangle between the herd and the cliff. When all was ready the hidden Indians stepped forth and frightened the grazing buffalo by walking toward them, waving blankets and yelling. The Indian disguised as a buffalo then led the way toward the precipice and at the last moment took refuge in a crevice as the front-running buffalo were forced over the brink by those behind. This picture of a large scale model of a "pishkun" indicates the crude and cruel methods utilized by primitive Indians of the gaunt and bitter plains in their battle for survival.

Photo: Montana Museum of History

Village Dwellers of the Southwest

In the hot, arid Southwest, Indians lived in compact villages and cultivated the land along the few rivers and streams, raising corn and also cotton, which they had learned to weave into cloth. The village dwellers were relatively peaceful, home-loving people who excelled in such handicrafts as pottery and basket making. When the white man introduced wool and beads, Indians quickly learned to use them in making beautiful blankets and ornamental beadwork. Some of the more adventurous village dwellers, among them the Navahos and Apaches, became nomadic herdsmen after the arrival of the Spanish made horses available.

Print: National Archives

Seed Gatherers of the Arid West

Before the arrival of the white man, the Indians of California and the Great Basin eked out an austere existence in that dry and almost barren land grubbing for seeds and acorns and endeavoring to snare an occasional rabbit, deer, or fish to augment their meager diet. They knew nothing of irrigation or the rudiments of cultivation. Their homes were miserable hovels made of brush; their clothing, of braided sagebrush. Their only real skill was basket weaving.

Fishermen of the Northwest

Of all the American Indians, those living along the northwest Pacific coast probably lived better and with less effort than did any other group. A year's supply of food could be obtained within a few weeks when salmon swarmed up the rivers from the ocean. In addition, the forests abounded in all sorts of game, berries, and herbs, and also provided the western red cedar which was easily converted with crude Indian tools of stone or horn into canoes or rough boards for building houses. Furs were used for winter clothing, and weaving of goat hair and other material was done. Occasionally raids were made against these people by the more warlike tribes from farther north and the captives made slaves; however, this was rare and constituted practically the only instance of slavery among the North American tribes.

Photo: Smithsonian Institution

Model of Norse Boat Such as Leif Ericson Used

It seems probable that the first Europeans to reach the North American continent were Norse sailors led by Leif Ericson about A.D. 1000. Because they found grapes growing along the shores of the new country they named it Vineland.

Depicted is a model of a Viking ship patterned after one unearthed in a "king's burial mound" near Sandefjord, Norway, in 1880 and now on display in the Royal Frederick University at Oslo. The original boat made during the Leif Ericson era had an over-all length of 67 feet, was 17 feet wide amidship, and had a depth of 4 feet. The sturdy craft, made of one-inch oak planking held in place by iron nails, was calked with oakum made of cow's hair. There were thirty-two oars, each 20 feet long; the single mast had a square sail, and the open deck was floored with loose planks. Crew members hung their shields on the gunwales while rowing, and during bad weather a red and white tent cloth made of fine woolen material was stretched overhead. Also found were wooden bunks, dishes, and related articles essential to such a voyage.

Photo: Smithsonian Institution

Columbus Discovers a New World

Little change resulted from the visit of the Norsemen, and five hundred years passed before an Italian named Christopher Columbus, sailing west in 1492 under the flag of Spain in search of a water route to Japan and India, discovered a whole new world. Landing on a group of islands in the Caribbean, he claimed them for Spain and, thinking he was near India, called the natives "Indians"—a misnomer probably never to be corrected. Columbus made several trips to Central and South America, but he never reached the northern mainland nor knew of its existence. Although it is true that "he did not know where he was going when he started, did not know where he was when he got there, and did not know where he had been when he got back," his place in history is secure. Like so many great men, Columbus was not fully appreciated by his contemporaries and he died a poverty-stricken and lonely old man, unaware of the magnitude of his accomplishments.

Print: National Archives

Discovery of North America by John and Sebastian Cabot

In 1497 and again in 1498, another Italian, John Cabot, with his son Sebastian, sailing under the English flag, cruised along the coast of North America and claimed it for England. About the same time still another Italian, Amerigo Vespucci, sailing for the Portuguese, touched the coast of the southern continent and, because of the widespread reading of his published letters, his name was applied to North and South America.

Print: Library of Congress

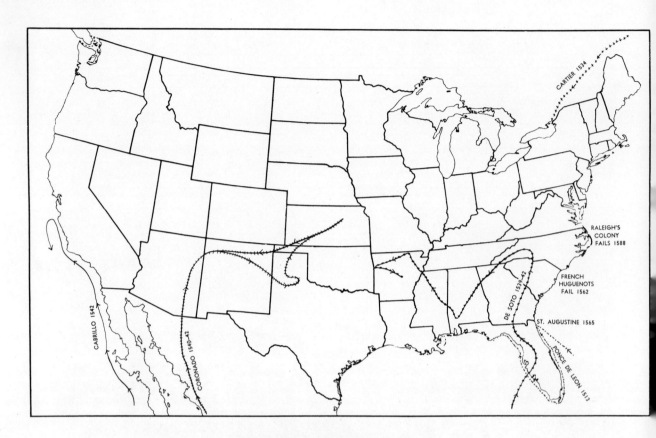

The First Hundred Years
1500–1600

III. THE FIRST HUNDRED YEARS—1500–1600

SPAIN, ENGLAND AND FRANCE EXPLORE—FRENCH AND ENGLISH COLONIES FAIL—SPAIN RETAINS A TOEHOLD

During the New World's first century, that is, from around 1500 to 1600, activity was concerned primarily with exploration, fortune hunting, and missionary work. The homemaker and farmer had little part in the doings of that early period. Ponce de León discovered Florida, De Soto roamed over the southeastern part of the United States, Coronado over the southwest, and Cabrillo (1542) cruised along the coast of California, but none found the gold they sought. The French touched at New York harbor (1524), Cartier (1534) sailed up the St. Lawrence, and the Huguenots (1562) sought unsuccessfully to establish a refuge in South Carolina and Florida. The English, under Sir Walter Raleigh's guidance, strove to establish a settlement on Roanoke Island, North Carolina (1587), but the people of this colony disappeared, never to be heard from again. A century drifted by leaving hardly a trace of the European visits.

Ponce de León Seeks the Fountain of Youth

The modern story of North America begins with Ponce de León, a Spaniard sent in 1513 to capture an "island" northwest of Puerto Rico, on which there was rumored to be a fountain whose waters gave perpetual youth. He named the land Florida and searched diligently but without success for the fabulous fountain.

Print: Library of Congress

Spanish Fort in Florida

A quarter of a century after the coming of Ponce de León another Spaniard, Hernando de Soto, began his wanderings throughout the South which ended three years later when he died and was buried in the Mississippi River. After one hundred and thirty years, the Spanish erected this old fort at St. Augustine, Florida, which withstood many furious assaults and was never captured until Gary Cooper accomplished the feat in one of his movies. The gold of the southern regions, especially Mexico and Peru, lured the Spanish away from the northern mainland and restricted their activities in the north for decades, by which time it was too late for them to prevent the establishing of other European colonies.

St. Augustine, Fla., Chamber of Commerce Photo by Harris

F. GERITZ

Juan Rodríguez Cabrillo

Discoverer of California

Pushing exploration of the New World in all directions by both land and sea, Spain dispatched Juan Rodriguez Cabrillo (a Portuguese) up the outer coast of Lower California in 1542, and in June of that year he dropped anchor in San Diego Bay, thereby becoming the first European to visit what is now the state of California. Cabrillo died the next year but Ferrelo, his pilot, continued up the West Coast as far north as the Rogue River area of Oregon.

Print: California State Library

The Coming of the Horse

Bold and adventurous men of Spain were the first Europeans to see the West, and in 1540–42 Coronado explored parts of Arizona, New Mexico, northern Texas, and Kansas in a futile search for cities reputed to be rich in gold. The Spaniards brought with them the first horses to be seen in the Western Hemisphere since prehistoric times, and as Coronado wandered over the Southwest many of his horses strayed or were stolen from his herd. These animals became the foundation stock from which developed, over the succeeding three hundred years, the wild, tough mustangs with which the Indians attacked the caravans of the pioneers.

Photo: U.S. Bureau of Public Roads

The Lost Colony,

Roanoke, North Carolina

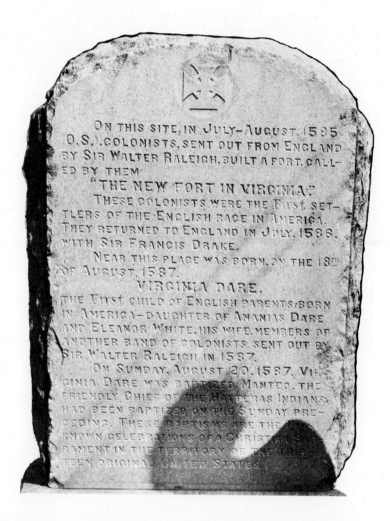

ON THIS SITE, IN JULY–AUGUST, 1585 (O.S.), COLONISTS, SENT OUT FROM ENGLAND BY SIR WALTER RALEIGH, BUILT A FORT, CALLED BY THEM

"THE NEW FORT IN VIRGINIA."

THESE COLONISTS WERE THE FIRST SETTLERS OF THE ENGLISH RACE IN AMERICA. THEY RETURNED TO ENGLAND IN JULY, 1586, WITH SIR FRANCIS DRAKE.

NEAR THIS PLACE WAS BORN, ON THE 18TH OF AUGUST, 1587,

VIRGINIA DARE,

THE FIRST CHILD OF ENGLISH PARENTS, BORN IN AMERICA—DAUGHTER OF ANANIAS DARE AND ELEANOR WHITE, HIS WIFE, MEMBERS OF ANOTHER BAND OF COLONISTS, SENT OUT BY SIR WALTER RALEIGH IN 1587.

ON SUNDAY, AUGUST 20, 1587, VIRGINIA DARE WAS BAPTIZED. MANTEO, THE FRIENDLY CHIEF OF THE HATTERAS INDIANS, HAD BEEN BAPTIZED ON THE SUNDAY PRECEDING. THESE BAPTISMS ARE THE FIRST KNOWN CELEBRATIONS OF A CHRISTIAN SACRAMENT IN THE TERRITORY OF THE THIRTEEN ORIGINAL UNITED STATES.

Among the first to look upon the New World as a place for colonization and homemaking rather than exploitation was the Englishman Sir Walter Raleigh. He planted a colony on Roanoke Island off the coast of North Carolina, but the settlers became discouraged and gladly accepted an offer from the roving Sir Francis Drake to return home. Raleigh persisted, however, and two years later, in 1587, he sent out about a hundred and twenty colonists, who were left stranded when England's attention was concentrated on the attack by the Spanish Armada. When a rescue ship finally arrived at Roanoke Island the settlers had disappeared, and their ill-fated project has gone down in history as the "Lost Colony." Although Raleigh's principal objective had failed, the enterprise had far-reaching results in that the idea of colonization was firmly implanted in Britain. Also, a great deal had been learned about the climate, soil, and other resources of the area, indicating the feasibility of establishing a flourishing agricultural community.

In 1600, the end of the First Hundred Years, there was not a single European to be found in the whole vast continent north of Florida. Although more than a century had elapsed since the coming of Columbus, the primeval forests, treeless plains, towering mountains, and snowbound North remained the haunt of wild animals and the home of savage Indians. From California to Alaska, from the Gulf of Mexico to the North Pole, from St. Augustine, Florida, to Labrador, no trace remained of the first visits of the English, Spanish, and French.

Photo: North Carolina News Bureau

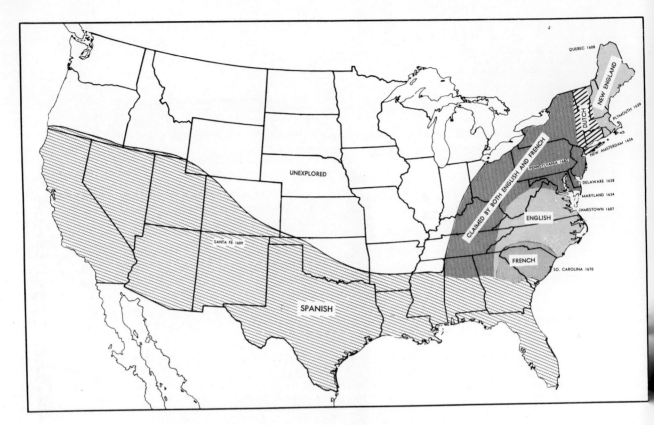

QUEBEC 1608
NEW ENGLAND
DUTCH
PLYMOUTH 1620
NEW AMSTERDAM 1626
CLAIMED BY BOTH ENGLISH AND FRENCH
PENNSYLVANIA 1682
DELAWARE 1638
MARYLAND 1634
JAMESTOWN 1607
ENGLISH
UNEXPLORED
FRENCH
SO. CAROLINA 1670
SANTA FE 1609
SPANISH

Colonization During Second Hundred Years
1600–1700

IV. THE SECOND HUNDRED YEARS—1600-1700

HOMEMAKING SETTLERS ARRIVE—THE STRUGGLE FOR SURVIVAL—THE FOUNDATIONS ARE LAID

Perhaps the most significant event in the entire history of the New World occurred at the beginning of the second century after Columbus. This was the arrival of English families whose whole purpose was to create a home in the wilderness for themselves and their posterity. These plain people, poorly educated and with meager resources, were not seeking gold or fame or excitement—they were homemakers, but in their slow, "inefficient," undramatic way, they constituted an irresistible force which conquered a continent and created a Nation out of a hostile wilderness.

The homemakers' first hundred years were a constant struggle for survival—a struggle against awful plagues, savage Indians, bitter weather, the overwhelming wilderness, homesickness, conflicting interests, and conniving governments. A struggle to learn how to live in a strange and unfriendly land, how to build a comfortable house, how to clear the land of rocks, trees, and brush, what crops to grow and how to grow them, what to produce for sale in England to provide the manufactured goods so sorely needed, how to get along with neighbors of vastly different religious, political, social, and economic views, how to establish law and order under regulations laid down by uninformed rulers thousands of miles away. The first century was a period of trial and error under heartbreaking conditions where toil and trouble were the daily lot of courageous people. The hardships and privations of the 17th century pioneers are indicated by their short span of life. Tombstones in old cemeteries tell the tale—only a rugged few lived the Biblical four score and ten and most were old at 30 and in their graves at 40. Despite the hazards and rigors of the pioneers, the number of emigrants steadily increased and by 1700 the population had grown from a handful at Jamestown in 1607 to more than 275,000. Many who came were indentured servants, that is, they pledged their labor for seven years in return for passage and assistance in getting started on their own when their period of service, which carried no social stigma, was completed. Others bought small tracts of land and as they prospered added to their acreage or sold out and moved further inland where cheaper land was available. Gold had supported the early Spanish in Central and South America, but English colonists found no quantity of gold although they excitedly sent a shipload of glittering material to England only to learn that it was worthless mica. Furs, deerskins, tall timber for ship masts, tar, pitch, turpentine, tobacco, fishing, and ship building were the basic commodities and enterprises which sustained the English colonies until a more diversified economy could be developed.

Jamestown, Virginia,

the First English Colony, 1607

The start of colonization was a tiny English settlement at Jamestown, Virginia, in 1607, followed in 1609 by the Spanish outpost Santa Fe in New Mexico; the Plymouth Colony in Massachusetts in 1620; the Dutch in New Amsterdam (New York) in 1626, when Peter Minuit bought Manhattan Island from the Indians for $24; the efforts of the Calverts to set up a manorial system in Maryland in 1634; the short-lived settlement in 1638 of New Sweden in Delaware which was taken over by New Amsterdam in 1655; the establishment of Charleston, South Carolina, in 1670 and the beginning of the plantation system; the arrival in 1682 of William Penn, son of a British admiral, with a Royal Grant to the land which later became Pennsylvania, and the settlement on Matagorda Bay in 1685. There were two types of English colonies, the company-operated and the individually owned. Those sponsored by private companies authorized by a charter from the King for trading purposes included Virginia, New York, Massachusetts, and Delaware. Those established by influential friends of a monarch were Maryland, New Hampshire, New Jersey, the Carolinas, Pennsylvania, and Georgia.

Photo: National Park Service

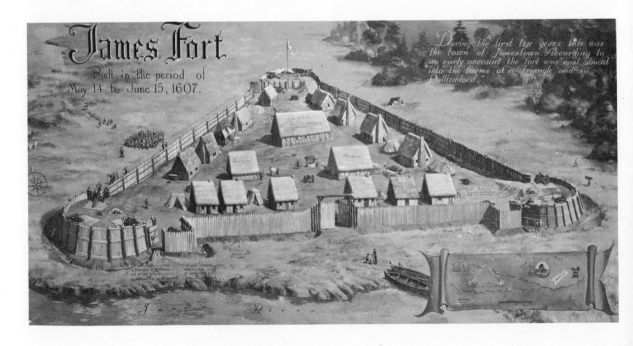

Old Church at Jamestown, Virginia

The British were slow in colonizing activities because of preoccupation with home affairs and threatening dangers from the Continent. Following the defeat of the Spanish Armada in 1588, the English again turned their attention to lands overseas. Sir Walter Raleigh's efforts to establish a colony proved fruitless; however in 1607, with the aid of a group of London businessmen, Jamestown in Virginia was founded. At the outset the agreement was that everybody would work and share in the community effort. However, human nature being what it is, the lazy and incompetent frustrated the project until the right of each individual to profit by his own efforts provided the necessary stimulus for strenuous activity. The colony profited by the energy and ability of Captain John Smith, and its success was assured when John Rolfe, who married Pocahontas, daughter of an Indian chief, developed a method for handling tobacco which made its shipment to Europe profitable. The only remaining evidence of early Jamestown above ground is this ivy-covered Old Church Tower and its sturdy walls, now over three hundred years old. The Church of England was dominant in the South in early times, but it never controlled the government nor set up a theocracy as the Puritan group did for a period in New England. Aided in England by the brilliant and liberal Sir Edwin Sandys, Jamestown became the first colony to enjoy local self-government.

Photo: Virginia State Chamber of Commerce

39

Henry Hudson

Descending the Hudson River

More than a century after discovery of the New World, explorers were still seeking a water route around North America that would lead directly to China and the rich spice islands of the Far East. Rumor persisted that there was a northwest passage connecting the Atlantic and the Pacific, and many expeditions searched fruitlessly for a ship lane which actually did not exist. In 1609, Henry Hudson, an Englishman sailing under the Dutch flag, searched the North Atlantic coast for the elusive water gap and discovered the river now bearing his name. Hudson made friends with the Iroquois Indians and laid the foundation for the profitable fur trade and other commercial activities of the Dutch West India Company.

Print: Library of Congress

The Shot That Cost France an Empire, 1609

Samuel de Champlain, intrepid French explorer, drew the below sketch of an incident in which he was the principal actor and which foreshadowed the loss of France's vast possessions in North America. In 1608 Champlain built a fort at Quebec and, viewing the forests and rich land stretching away to the south and west to be had for the taking, he dreamed of establishing a great French empire in America. The next year, in furtherance of his plans, he joined the Algonquin Indians in a war against their ancient enemies, the mighty Iroquois of the New York and Ohio country. At the outset of the attack Champlain and two of his aides fired their guns, killing two Iroquois chiefs and frightening the other warriors so badly that they fled in terror. The Iroquois fighting men had never seen nor heard of such awesome weapons, but they quickly regained their courage and vowed eternal hostility against the French. During the ensuing one hundred and fifty years the Iroquois fought the French bitterly, hampering their efforts at colonization, disrupting the fur trade, and preventing movement south from Canada into the Hudson Valley and beyond. In the long and desperate struggle between the French and English the powerful Iroquois aided the latter, causing the French to rue the day that Champlain fired the shot that lost an empire.

Print: Champlain Society, Toronto, Canada

The Tobacco-Rolling Road

By 1619 the Jamestown colony, after twelve years of trial and error, was firmly established, with tobacco assuring a profitable export trade. A Dutch ship left a number of Negroes at Jamestown a year before the landing of the Pilgrims at Plymouth and more than a decade before the Puritans arrived at Massachusetts Bay. Although they were to be followed by generations of emigrants from all parts of the world, Negroes were the only group to come here against their will. As production of tobacco spread, slave labor kept pace with it. Tobacco was an ideal crop along the coastal plain of the southern colonies because soil and climate were favorable and valuable crops could be produced among the stumps of small clearings in the forest. It could also be stored indefinitely, and it survived in good condition the long voyage to England, where it was in great demand. At first there was considerable natural open land and many fields that the Indians had cleared by burning off the forest, and these were early put into production. Then began the long, slow, laborious task of removing the trees which seemingly stretched out endlessly.

As tobacco culture moved inland, "rolling roads" were established over which heavy wooden hogsheads containing tobacco were rolled for a hundred miles or more to ports where sailing ships carried it abroad.

Photo: Bureau of Public Roads

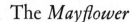

The *Mayflower*

In 1620, a group of English colonists dominated by religious dissenters en route to Virginia aboard the *Mayflower* got off their course and finally put ashore on the New England coast. Known as Pilgrims, they landed in December on a stern and rock-bound coast where winters were severe and prospects bleak. During the first winter half of the group of 102 men, women, and children died of disease and exposure, and when spring came about all they had left was faith and courage. But this was enough, and when the *Mayflower* departed for the return trip to England not one of the little band gave up and went home.

Many of the dissenters had lived for several years in Holland, where they had been made welcome by the friendly and tolerant Dutch, but, realizing that their little group of Englishmen would soon lose its identity, they decided to set sail for the New World and there establish a community of their own liking.

Businessmen in England joined with the Pilgrims in an unincorporated joint stock enterprise under which the emigrants were to work without pay for seven years, receiving supplies on a share and share alike basis. This arrangement proved as unworkable as the earlier one at Jamestown, and it was abandoned for a system in which each person prospered according to his talents and energy. Americans are often depicted as being primarily concerned with material things, but it is a curious fact that in this country one of the most coveted honors is to be able to say that your ancestors came over in the *Mayflower*—the battered little ship that probably had aboard the most poverty-stricken group ever to reach these shores. Because of succeeding generations almost a million Americans can now rightfully claim kinship to the *Mayflower* group.

Photo: Library of Congress

43

Chief Massasoit,
Friend of the Pilgrims

The arrival of the Pilgrims was greeted with mixed reactions by the Indians of New England, but fortunately Chief Massasoit of the nearest tribe proved friendly. Massasoit's aid, advice, and instruction in growing crops and overcoming the hazards of the wilderness made it possible throughout his lifetime for the struggling colony to survive. Indian resistance was minimized by the fact that a horrible smallpox plague, three years before the landing of the Pilgrims, had greatly reduced their numbers and left them in such a weakened condition that they were themselves struggling to exist.

Photo: The Dickson's, Plymouth, Mass.

Pilgrim Dugouts

According to certain widely publicized paintings, the Pilgrims lived in log cabins built of horizontal logs with notched ends, but crude dugout shelters with sides of upright logs like these were the nearest the pioneer Pilgrims came to building a home resembling the familiar log cabin of later years. Miserable huts with turf roofs, rough floors, and windows of oiled paper were the homes of these brave people who, together with their Indian friends, celebrated the First Thanksgiving a year after they stepped ashore on Plymouth Rock.

Photo: National Archives

English Wigwams

In addition to the log dugout, the so-called "English wigwam" was a familiar home in the early years of the colonies. An adaptation of the Indian wigwam, it consisted of a frame of hickory saplings covered with mats woven from cattail rushes over which was laid pine bark stripped from logs. Rushes were also used for floor covering. A fireplace of field stone joined with mortar made by pulverizing clam and oyster shells was placed at one end of the structure. At the opposite end of the room was a wooden door with a latch which was operated by a leather string that passed through a small hole in the door. At night, or when intruders were feared, the latch string was pulled inside, but at other times it hung outside, thus giving rise to the friendly invitation, "Come to see me; the latch string is out."

Photo: Pioneer Village, Salem, Mass.

Thatched-Roof Homes

of the Pilgrims

A more substantial and comfortable home is typified by the frame weatherboarded house with thatched roof shown below. The hand-sawed boards were held in place by handmade nails. The thatched roof was made by overlapping bundles of rye straw tied to rafters and intervening poles. Once in place, the thatch was combed and trimmed. Such houses had wooden floors, a loft reached by a ladder, removable windows of oiled paper protected by wooden shutters with leather hinges, and a field-stone fireplace. Unfortunately, the immediate need for houses often resulted in freshly cut lumber being used, and after a few months of weathering the boards warped and twisted, drawing the house out of shape and allowing icy winds to whistle through the cracks.

Photo: Plymouth, Mass., Chamber of Commerce

New Amsterdam

The Dutch West India Company established a fur-trading post in 1621 on the tip of an island at the mouth of the Hudson River where there was a magnificent harbor. The colony expanded as large grants of land were made along the river and baronial holdings established. New Amsterdam, as depicted here in 1660, was a prosperous town with broad streets, substantial buildings, and comfortable homes and formal parks. Inland, at the north end of town, a wall was built for protection against attack; later this became Wall Street—principal financial section in the City of New York. Beyond Wall Street were the farms, or

"boweries," of the Dutch farmers. The ten thousand Dutch colonists worked hard to develop their commercial enterprise and carried on a running fight with the Spanish which greatly hampered that nation in its struggle with England. Leading off to the north was a wide street which now is Broadway.

In 1664 New Amsterdam fell to the British and the name was changed to New York.

Photo: Museum of the City of New York

Governor Endicott of Massachusetts Bay Colony

Ten years after the hardy little band of Pilgrims landed at Plymouth, another group of dissenters from the Church of England arrived in Massachusetts. These people called themselves "Puritans" to signify that, unlike the Pilgrims who had separated entirely from the Church of England, they desired to stay within the Church but to purify it of worldly ways and what they considered outmoded trappings. Also, unlike the impoverished Pilgrims, the Puritans were relatively well-to-do, were well backed financially, had capable leaders who planned carefully and were allowed to bring their charter with them, permitting the colony nearly complete self-rule. Further, the initial group was followed within a year by more than a thousand emigrants and within ten years (1640) twenty-five thousand Puritans, spurred on by persecution and difficult times in England, had arrived to make the Massachusetts Bay Colony dominant in New England.

Photo: Library of Congress

Maryland Manor

The third English colony was established in 1634 in Maryland in accordance with a charter given George Calvert, the first Lord Baltimore, who had attempted a similar but futile project on the icy shores of New-foundland. Calvert died while preparations were still under way, but his son Cecilius followed his father's ideas in directing the affairs of the Maryland colony. The proprietary charter granted to the Calverts by James I was generous, allowing great freedom of action and providing for a representative government. Lord Baltimore was a wise and forbearing man who, in making plans for his colony, resisted the intolerance of the times and welcomed various faiths as, when Secretary of State in England, he had favored admission of Separatists and others to Virginia. Although Catholics were particularly solicited for the

Maryland colony, relatively few responded, and from the outset (possibly even in the first group) people of other religious faiths predominated. A feudal system was contemplated wherein tracts of one thousand acres or more were to be known as manors and titles of nobility handed down, but this effort failed. Profiting by knowledge acquired from the Indians and by the grueling experiences of the Virginians, especially in the production of tobacco, the Maryland settlers fared well from the start. Neither the first Lord Baltimore nor his son Cecil, who succeeded him, ever resided in Maryland. The house shown here was built on Chesapeake Bay in southern Maryland in 1652 by Christopher Rousby and is similar to Greenway Court, occupied by Lord Fairfax in Virginia. The house is now in Greenfield Village, Dearborn, Michigan.

Photo: Henry Ford Museum, Dearborn, Mich.

Roger Williams,

Founder of Rhode Island

Although the Puritans had many admirable qualities, including sincerity, integrity, courage, thrift, and energy, their narrow "I'm right—you're wrong" form of religion lacked general appeal and was doomed to failure in the friendly, tolerant, democratic atmosphere that in time developed in this country and now enables some three hundred religious sects to prosper in peace and harmony.

Roger Williams, a young Puritan minister, was banned from the Massachusetts Bay Colony because of his belief that a person should not be compelled to support a church in which he did not believe. Williams fled through winter snows to friendly Indians, bought land from them, and in 1636 founded the town of Providence, which became the capital of Rhode Island, a state that helped establish the pattern of a liberal and enlightened society.

Photo: Architect of the Capitol

The Famous Log College

at Neshaminy, Pennsylvania

The first college in the United States was Harvard University, founded in 1636, followed by other church schools such as William and Mary (1693), Yale (1701), and the nonsectarian University of Pennsylvania in 1740. Depicted here is the famous Log College founded in 1736 in Bucks County, Pennsylvania, by the Reverend William Tennent, whose graduates established many other colleges, including Princeton University (1746), Hampden-Sidney (1776), and Washington College (now Washington and Lee) in 1749. The Log College, which was an educational center for more than a century, was established primarily as a theological seminary and emphasized instruction in Latin, Greek, Hebrew, and Christian doctrine.

Print: Bucks County Historical Society

The Log Cabin,

a Gift from the Swedes

One of the great contributions of colonial Swedes to the development of the United States was the one-room log cabin. Easily and quickly erected by a few men, built entirely of local materials (logs cut from forests and sealed with common clay) warm in winter and cool in summer, a fortress that endured a lifetime, the log cabin was a powerful factor in the settlement of the frontier. It was thirty years after the founding of Jamestown before houses of this type were built in the colonies and it was another thirty years before they came into general use along the Atlantic Coast. Once established, however, the log cabin became the typical pioneer home during the following years of westward expansion.

In more settled areas it was possible to provide windows of glass and fireplaces of brick, like these in an old cabin preserved in a Wilmington, Delaware, museum. In the wilderness, glass panes were replaced by animal skins or oiled paper. Chimneys and fireplaces were made of field-stones or logs plastered over with clay. Floors were often the bare earth, packed hard, or split logs with flat side up or, in more affluent cabins, rough hewn boards.

Photo: Delaware State Archives

First Printing Press in America

In 1640 this old press was used by Stephen Day in Cambridge, Massachusetts, to print the first book published in America, *The Book of Psalms,* sometimes referred to as the *Bay Psalm Book.* The *Bible, Pilgrim's Progress,* and almanacs were long the principal reading material available. In 1704 the first newspaper in America, the Boston *News-Letter,* was published. Over the years freedom of the press became a basic and lasting principle of American democracy. Books, magazines, and newspapers now roll from the presses regulated only by the laws of libel, decency, supply, and demand. There are currently published about two thousand privately owned newspapers, ten thousand weekly newspapers, and eight thousand magazines.

Photo: Vermont Historical Society

Water Power in the Old Days

Settlement followed the many rivers and streams which provided easy transportation and whose banks held rich soils. Along the coast, large rivers such as the Savannah, James, Potomac, Susquehanna, and Delaware offered miles of navigable waters for ships to go inland a hundred miles or so to the "fall line" where a sharp break in elevation between the Piedmont Plateau and the Coastal Plains creates falls in the rivers coming down from higher land. At such points "falls cities" grew up, such as Philadelphia, Baltimore, Washington, Richmond, Raleigh, Columbia, and Augusta. Along these rivers, farms or large plantations developed with direct trade with the mother country. Beyond the "fall line" were numerous streams which allowed small river boats to go even further inland. The rivers and streams also provided water power to operate mills used for grinding grain and sawing timber, depending on their location in regard to crops or timber. Since roads connecting the settlements strung out along the Atlantic Coast were few, practically impassable most of the year, and always dangerous because of Indians and bandits, travel between the colonies was not common. The colonies in the lower South were further isolated by frequent storms off Cape Hatteras which made it easier and safer for sailing vessels from South Carolina and Georgia to go to Europe than to New England.

Photo: USDA by Forsythe

A Dog-Trot House

Throughout the South, when a one-room log cabin became too crowded, another just like it was built some ten or twelve feet to one side and the two buildings were joined by a roof. The space between was sometimes left in bare earth, but more commonly it was floored with halved logs or thick boards, forming a breezeway which was the family gathering place during long hot summers. The open area was such a favorite haunt of the dogs that a double log house of this type became known as a "dog-trot" or "dog-run" house. As the owner prospered, the breezeway was likely to be walled in to make a hall or an additional room. From such humble beginnings developed the center entrance hall of the mansions of the "Cotton Kingdom." Although this house was built in the Indian Territory far beyond the Alleghenies, it is an excellent example of the various phases through which the log cabin passed in its rise from humble backwoods home to Southern mansion. The wing, or ell, running to the rear at one side represents a further step in the development of a typical house of a later period.

Photo: Oklahoma Historical Society

A Compact New England House

Because of the long cold winters, Northern houses were almost the exact opposite of those developed in the South. Instead of large rooms, high ceilings, wide halls, and spacious verandas designed to provide comfort in hot and humid country, the Northern houses had relatively small, compact, easy-to-heat rooms, gable roofs, small windows, huge fireplaces with chimneys in the center of the house to utilize the warmth, and often no porch at all. By 1664, sturdy, comfortable, and commodious houses like this one in Portsmouth, New Hampshire, (above) were being built in the northern colonies. *Photo: National Archives*

A Seventeenth Century Virginia Brick House

Between 1636 and 1640, Adam Thoroughgood built this attractive and comfortable brick house (below) on his Virginia tract of over five thousand acres which he had been given in return for having procured the importation of 105 persons. The house has four rooms, two on each floor, with a spacious center hall, thus revealing its kinship to the "dog-trot" house.

A few years ago a trap door was discovered in the north bedroom, close to the chimney, opening into a secret passage which led down to the river. Such secret exits were common in early colonial homes because of the danger from Indians and other marauders. *Photo: Virginia Chamber of Commerce*

Marquette and Joliet

Explore the

"Father of Waters,"

1673

Restless Frenchmen in Montreal, Canada, eagerly probed farther west, hoping to find the elusive Northwest Passage. Among them were the missionary, Marquette, and the trader, Joliet, who shared curiosity as to what lay beyond the next hill or around the next bend of the river. Enticed by rumors of a great river, called by the Indians the "Father of Waters," the intrepid pair in 1673 worked their way west by stream and portage until they reached the Wisconsin River, which led their frail canoes into the mighty Mississippi River. Enchanted by the lush fields of what are now Iowa and Illinois, the abundance of game and wildlife along the shores, and the friendly Indians, they drifted south as far as present-day Arkansas. Then, fearing capture by the Spanish or hostile Indians and convinced they had not found the Northwest Passage, they turned back and came home by a "short cut" up the Illinois River.

Photo: Library of Congress

La Salle Goes All the Way down the Mississippi, 1682

In 1682 the explorer La Salle was the first to follow the Mississippi River all the way to its mouth. He envisioned a great inland empire for his beloved France, but he was killed before being able to develop plans. However, the strategic importance of controlling the entrance to the Mississippi was recognized and a race between the British, French, and Spanish to establish a post there got under way in 1699. Two brothers, Sieur de Iberville and Sieur de Bienville, won by founding Biloxi, Mississippi, followed by a few other small outposts in the valley. Their situation was precarious since there were only a handful of Frenchmen scattered over the valley as compared to nearly three hundred thousand English colonists along the Atlantic coast. At Iberville's back were the Spanish, ready to pounce upon him at the first sign of weakness, and there was always the danger of an Indian uprising. Yet somehow he and his struggling little community survived. Finally, in 1718, more than a century after Jamestown, a place named New Orleans was laid out near the mouth of the river. Strenuous efforts of the French government to build up their tightly controlled settlements in the Louisiana Territory failed largely because few families came to make permanent homes in that raw and undeveloped country. The French pursued the alluring fur trade and, like the Spanish, gave only secondary attention to agricultural development, although later a few large indigo plantations were established and still later sugar cane and cotton were introduced, becoming important following the Louisiana Purchase.

Photo: U.S. Bureau of Public Roads

William Penn Dealing with Indians, 1681

William Penn, son of a noted British admiral, became a convert to the Quaker faith while a student at Oxford and, despite imprisonment and the objections of his father, he stood steadfast in his belief. The admiral had lent the King sixteen thousand pounds, and to settle this debt the young Quaker in 1681 was given a royal grant to the land between New York and Maryland in which to establish a refuge for members of his faith. Penn was highly intelligent, a great organizer, liberal in his political, religious, and social views, energetic and resourceful, and fair and honest in his dealings with the Indians and others. As a consequence, Pennsylvania thrived, becoming the home of people from many countries and of many different creeds.

Print: National Archives

South Carolina Rice Plantation, 1714

At Charleston, South Carolina, in 1670 a group of English noblemen backed an attempt to set up a colony comprising large landed estates. The following year the group was joined by another band of English settlers from Barbados, who brought with them a knowledge of the plantation system of farming. However, their most important exports for the next two decades were furs and deerskins obtained from Indians by traders on horseback who bartered their way through the forests all the way to the Mississippi River. In the meantime planters experimented vigorously with cattle and hogs and such crops as indigo, cotton, tea, olives, oranges, grapes, and silk. Rice culture got its start in America when a sailing ship, blown off its course in 1685, by chance put in at Charleston for repairs and a bag of rice was given to a planter, Dr. Henry Woodward. The crop flourished in the swampy lands of the area, and through the use of slave labor there arose a wealthy plantation class that dominated the community for decades. Upcountry, the development of small pioneer farms followed the pattern of the frontier elsewhere. Subjected to attacks by the Spanish, French, Indians, and pirates, the South Carolina colonists became strong, determined, self-sufficient, and rugged individualists. A representative form of government and religious toleration attracted emigrants, including many French Huguenots, and by 1700 the colony had a population of more than five thousand. The stalwart brick house shown here was built in 1714 on a rice plantation along the Cooper River, near Charleston. It was used as a stronghold during the Yamassee Indian War in 1715 and was occupied by the British during the Revolution. Such places were relatively few, but their owners were usually prominent in the community's social, political, and economic affairs. In time, ownership of a plantation became almost a social necessity in Charleston, even for doctors and lawyers who otherwise had no interest in farming.

Photo: South Carolina Research Planning and Development Board

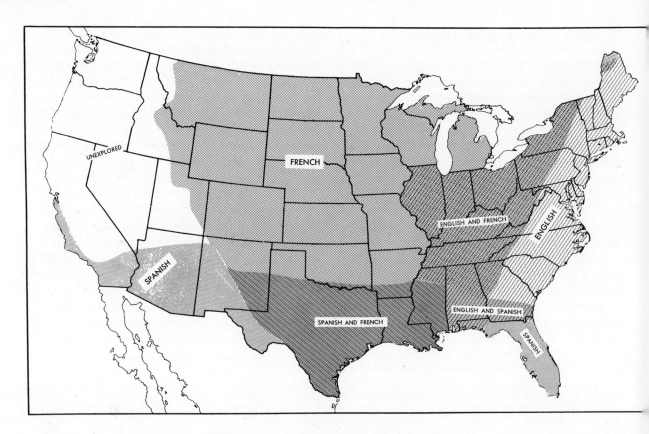

UNEXPLORED

FRENCH

SPANISH

ENGLISH AND FRENCH

ENGLISH

SPANISH AND FRENCH

ENGLISH AND SPANISH

SPANISH

European Claims About 1700

V. THE THIRD HUNDRED YEARS—1700–1800

EUROPEAN EFFORTS TO SEIZE AND TO HOLD
AMERICA—BEGINNINGS OF PROSPERITY—RISING
TIDE OF INDEPENDENCE—A NEW NATION IS
BORN—WESTWARD HO!

The tiny English settlements strung like beads on a string along the Atlantic coast slowly gained strength and by 1700 had a population of 275,000 not counting 5,000 Negroes and an undetermined number of Indians. During the century just closed, the line of frontier settlement had moved west roughly a hundred miles. The momentum thus generated, fed by steadily increasing immigration, rising prices and expanding trade, brought about the beginnings of prosperity after a century of bare subsistence, and laid the foundations for a tremendous upsurge in the economic life of the colonies during the 18th century. The establishment of newspapers, improved roads, mail service and kindred improvements not only helped business but also brought the colonies closer together than they had been previously, although they were still seriously hampered by the lack of good inter-colony transportation and of a sound and uniform currency. Some of the more energetic and talented colonists accumulated considerable wealth. Merchants, shippers, and professional people prospered and the seacoast towns shared in the general rise in the standard of living but in the back country and on the frontier, conditions were little changed. This disparity between the settled "East" and the frontier "West" was to continue for nearly 200 years and cause many difficulties.

England had founded the colonies primarily as a source of raw materials and to provide an outlet for her manufactured products. This system was well maintained in the South as tobacco, rice, indigo, naval stores, and hides found a ready market in England. The surplus grain and other food products of the middle colonies also were welcome but most of the exportable items of New England were not greatly needed in Great Britain, so those colonies looked elsewhere for markets. In the West Indies, lumber, meat,

grain, and fish from New England were exchanged for molasses, sugar, fruit and the like which were traded in England for manufactured goods needed in the colonies. Similar three-cornered trade deals were worked out with North Africa. Meanwhile, the French had moved light forces into the Mississippi Valley and laid claim to a vast area west of the Allegheny Mountains. In Europe, age-old rivalries and struggles for power continued unabated and each of these wars had their actions overseas. North American activities in these European wars have too often been thought of as dissociated events and simply isolated colonial wars. The fact is that the so-called King William's War, 1689–97, was merely one phase of the War of the League of Augsburg. Likewise, Queen Anne's War, 1702–13, was the American counterpart of the War of the Spanish Succession, and King George's War, 1744–48, was similarly related to the War of the Austrian Succession. The French and Indian War, 1754–63, was the American phase of the world wide "Seven Years' War."

During America's third hundred years (1700–1800), the long and bloody struggle for possession of North America reached a climax between the British, French, Indians, and the colonists. In the end it was the colonists themselves who settled the issue by driving out the British, who had in turn driven out both the French and the Dutch, the latter having previously gobbled up the Swedes. There remained only the Spanish and the Indians but in the next century they, too, were to fall before the man with the plow and the long rifle. At the end of the third hundred years (by 1800), a new nation was born and more than 5,300,000 white people resided in the infant republic—a gain from 275,000 at the start of the century—and the pattern of the future began to take shape.

Governor's Palace at Williamsburg

When the State House at Jamestown burned in 1698 the Assembly voted to move farther inland to a location they called Williamsburg, and to erect there a new capitol building and other necessary structures, including a governor's house. In this palace, as it was called, built 1706–20, the royal governors entertained in the grand manner and set the style for "quality folk" throughout the tidewater area. Seven royal governors resided here, and also the first two governors of Virginia, Patrick Henry and Thomas Jefferson. The royal governors were appointed by the King, although they usually were paid by colonial legislatures, an arrangement conducive to "middle of the road" policies.

Photo: Colonial Williamsburg

The Governor's Formal Garden

The Ballroom Garden of the Governor's Palace is a thing of genuine beauty. Through the generosity of John D. Rockefeller, Jr., the entire town of Williamsburg has been restored to its colonial condition, including the Old Capitol building, taverns and shops, and the original jail.

Photo: Colonial Williamsburg

Colonial Capitol at Williamsburg

The English colonists clung tenaciously to the hard-won rights expressed in the Magna Carta and subsequent acts, and from the outset enjoyed representative government under the rule of a royal governor. In 1704 the Virginia Assembly moved into its new Capitol, the scene of many stirring events until 1779, when the seat of government was moved to Richmond, Virginia. In 1832 the Capitol was destroyed by fire a second time, and was reconstructed as shown at right in 1930.

Photo: Colonial Williamsburg

Virginia House of Burgesses, Training Ground for Self-Government

The House of Burgesses, where for over one hundred and fifty years representatives of the people met to consider legislation for governing the colony, was the training ground for many of the brilliant young men who were to lead the movement for independence and the founding of the new nation. Shown here is a reproduction of the chamber where George Washington and Thomas Jefferson served, and where their colleague Patrick Henry, the "Voice of the American Revolution," made a number of his fiery speeches. The colonies along the Atlantic coast enjoyed many privileges not found elsewhere in America, including trial by jury, free schools, a representative colonial government, a high degree of freedom of speech and religion.

Photo: Colonial Williamsburg

Stratford, Colonial Home of the Lees of Virginia

With the development of the plantation system in the tidewater region of Virginia, numerous beautiful mansions for wealthy landowners were constructed by expert architects brought over from England. These experts knew how to make the best use of the oak, walnut, yellow pine, maple, and poplar readily available on the plantations, together with bricks handmade by slaves. Homes were usually built on high ground along the many rivers used for local transportation and for shipping tobacco and other products. Most of the planters were slave owners. Stratford, the ancestral home of the Lees of Virginia, built 1729–30, was a product of the early colonial period when virgin soils and the tobacco boom supported such large estates.

Photo: Robert E. Lee Memorial Foundation, Inc.

General Oglethorpe, Founder of Georgia, 1733

The development of colonies along the Atlantic coast was a matter of great interest to forward-looking Englishmen. One of them, General James Edward Oglethorpe, portrayed above, was fearful that the Spanish would move northward from Florida, capturing the struggling colonies one at a time. To erect a barrier against such a possibility Oglethorpe, obtaining a charter from King George II, established a colony in 1733 which he named Georgia in honor of his sovereign. Savannah became the first permanent settlement in Georgia, where rum and slavery were prohibited. Oglethorpe built strong fortifications at strategic points, and, equally important, he neutralized the Indian menace by honest and skillful dealings with them. Through his strenuous and intelligent efforts the southern flank of the chain of English colonies was made secure.

Photo: Heriot, Savannah, Ga.

Forks of the Ohio River

As the English colonies prospered, added attention was given to the prospects of settlement beyond the mountains, especially in the country between the Great Lakes and the Ohio River. The French, claiming that area, maintained a number of outposts there from which they carried on a profitable fur trade. However, traders from Pennsylvania were also active in the northern sector where in 1753 the French started building a chain of forts connecting Lake Erie with the point at which the Allegheny and Monongahela rivers join to form the Ohio. As the French were building Fort Duquesne at the head of the Ohio, a colonial force led by the twenty-two-year-old George Washington was intercepted at hastily constructed Fort Necessity and defeated. Thus began the Seven Years' War, which ended with French defeat and the loss of their possessions in North America. Fort Duquesne became Fort Pitt and, in time, Pittsburgh. Situated due west from Philadelphia at the headwaters of the Ohio, which flows on to the Mississippi River in the Middle West, it was inevitable that Pittsburgh should become a busy trading center, shipping point, and reloading station after the great migration of pioneers into the Ohio country got under way.

Print: Smithsonian Institution

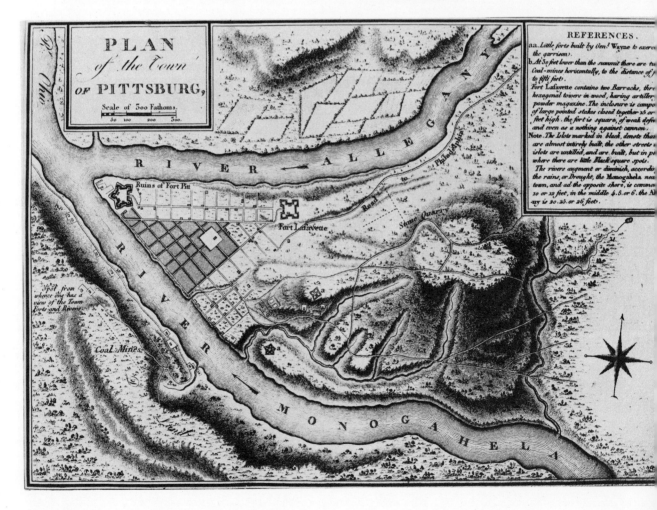

POSSESSIONS OF EUROPEAN STATES IN EASTERN NORTH AMERICA AFTER THE TREATY OF PARIS, 1763

When peace was restored in 1763, only two European nations retained possessions in North America, with the exception of Russian-held Alaska. The English had Canada and all of the area between the Atlantic Ocean and the Mississippi River. Spain had New Orleans and a tremendous domain beyond the Mississippi and west to the Pacific, peopled by Indian tribes and containing only a few struggling outposts in New Mexico. After more than a century and a half of bitter struggle, the French were eliminated from North America. Spain, having sided with the French during the late stages of the conflict, received from France the city of New Orleans and all of Louisiana west of the Mississippi, but she gave up Florida to the English.

Map: Carnegie Institute of Washington

Benjamin Franklin on the Boston Post Road, 1763

Benjamin Franklin (1706–90) was in many ways the most interesting and outstanding American of the eighteenth century. Born in Boston of poor parents, he was an apprentice printer at the age of twelve, and, like Washington, had little formal education and never attended college. Despite these handicaps, Franklin became the leading colonial literary figure of the century as well as an outstanding scientist, businessman, and statesman. Moving to Philadelphia (the "City of Brotherly Love") as a young man, Franklin helped found the first public library and the nonsectarian University of Pennsylvania, and he acquired the *Pennsylvania Gazette,* which later developed into the *Saturday Evening Post.* As a scientist Franklin is best known for his kite experiment, which demonstrated the connection between electricity and lightning. His *Autobiography* still makes good reading; his *Poor Richard's Almanack,* carrying news, weather information, proverbs, recipes, wise sayings, and a wealth of other information, was widely popular throughout the colonies. At the outbreak of the French and Indian War, Franklin presented a plan under which the thirteen colonies were to elect a central government to levy taxes and raise an army, but the project failed because the colonies distrusted each other and feared giving up even a part of their sovereignty to an "outside agency." He was a signer of the Declaration of Independence, and he urged its support by all the colonies, warning that, "We must all hang together or assuredly we shall all hang separately."

The versatile Franklin is here depicted traveling in a one-horse shay on an inspection tour of colonial post offices while he was Postmaster General. His daughter, on horseback, watches as a post rider delivers an urgent message to Franklin.

Photo: U.S. Bureau of Public Roads

Mount Vernon, Home of George Washington

All along the coast, from the Potomac south to the Savannah River, planters strove to lead the life of English squires, with big estates, fancy clothes, cultural avocations, and a foreign education. The accumulated wealth of more than a century of rising prices gave the wise, capable, and prudent a standard of living undreamed of by their poorer English forebears. The wealth of these country gentlemen allowed them leisure to participate in public affairs, and they became dominant in colonial legislatures, were prominent in the movement for independence, and provided many of the early presidents, cabinet members, and members of the Congress.

In 1754, George Washington, at the age of twenty-two, inherited a 2,500-acre plantation from a half brother. He devoted forty-five years to developing the house, grounds, and gardens of Mount Vernon despite long absences necessitated by his activities in the French and Indian War, the American Revolution, and the Presidency. The great strength of George Washington lay in his integrity, his unsurpassed executive ability, his solid common sense, his fairness to all, and his iron-willed determination to see a thing through to a successful conclusion. Then, as now, he was "first in war, first in peace, and first in the hearts of his countrymen."

Photo: National Archives

Daniel Boone, Frontiersman (1734–1820)

Boys raised on the frontier learned the ways of the wilderness as readily as Indian youths and became proficient in hunting, shooting, tracking, maintaining themselves alone in the dark and forbidding forests, and avoiding trouble with Indians or handling it when it arose. Daniel Boone, a Pennsylvania Quaker (1734–1820), throughout a long and adventurous life roamed a trackless and lonely wilderness where few if any white men had ventured. He labored to bring families to it to destroy the solitude and reduce the virgin forests to farm land and townsites. Drifting down the Shenandoah Valley to North Carolina with his family, he heard tales brought back by the "Long Hunters" of a wonderful land beyond the mountains and he determined to see it for himself. Dressed in the typical long deerskin hunting shirt and leather leggings with fringe attached, Indian moccasins on his feet, a knife at his belt, a small pouch for lead, salt, flints, a bullet mold, a powder horn over his shoulder, a coonskin cap on his head, and in his hands a long "Kentucky Rifle," Daniel Boone was ready for his two-year journey into the wilderness. In June, 1769, he and a few companions looked down from "Pilot's Knob" into Kentucky, "the dark and bloody ground" where Boone was to struggle hard and long to get rich by bringing in pioneer families to settle on land being sold by Richard Henderson and his Transylvania Company. A better woodsman than businessman, Boone lost his property and moved on to Missouri when it was still virgin territory and in his old age he greeted Meriwether Lewis and William Clark on their epochal journey across the continent to the far Northwest.

Down through the ages herds of buffalo, deer, bear, and other wild animals roamed about in search of food, water, and salt over the easiest grades and thus established the trails later followed successively by Indian, explorer, fur trader, hunter, and emigrant wagons, finally becoming broad highways and railroad beds. It was men such as Boone who searched out these trails and marked them for use in later years.

Photo: Copyright by Caulfield and Shook, Louisville, Ky.

72

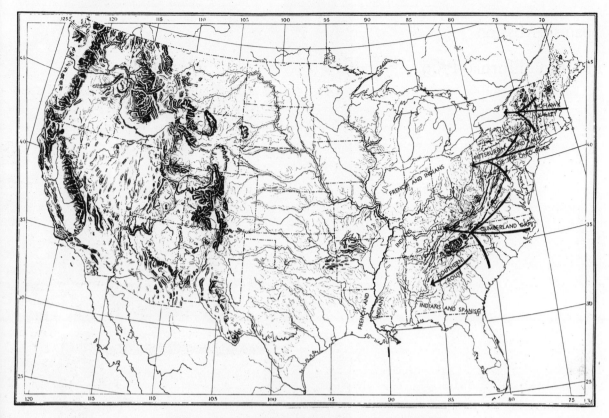

Main Routes Through Appalachian
Mountain Barriers in Colonial Period

Gateways to the West

The rugged tree-clad mountain range stretching a thousand miles from Maine to Georgia was for more than one hundred and fifty years a shield protecting the struggling little settlements along the coast from the ravages of the Indians of the interior. However, the time came when the Allegheny-Appalachian range was looked upon not so much as a shield but as a barrier to westward expansion.

By 1770 the English colonies had a population of over two million, most of them clustered along the Atlantic coast east of the Allegheny Mountains. Westward expansion had long been dreamed of, but practical considerations had restrained settlers who desired to leave poor and exhausted soils for the rich land which explorers and traders had described beyond the mountains. There were four principal gateways through this barrier to the West.

The route up the Mohawk Valley in central New York was level, short, and easily navigated, but it had been blocked by treaty with the Iroquois and by the embattled French who held the Great Lakes area.

In the center of the country the best way was along rivers and through natural gaps to the headwaters of the Ohio River, at Pittsburgh, but, as we have seen, the Ohio country had been held by the French and Indians, and after the Seven Years' War the British forbade settlement in an effort to avoid Indian trouble. A third route, and the one first used extensively, involved a long overland trek down the Shenandoah Valley of Virginia, over rough mountain trails through the Cumberland Gap, then by the Wilderness Road to central Kentucky and beyond. This route was long and hard and the territory to be settled swarmed with warlike Indians, but the settlers were inured to hardship and were determined they could handle the Indian problem. Far to the south at the lower end of the long mountain barrier there was level land of good quality and well watered, but this area had been closed by hostile Indians and the Spanish.

Spanish Mission
in Old California–1769

When the French gave up the Mississippi Valley to the English in 1763, the Spanish knew trouble was imminent. Scattered bands of carefree French hunters and trappers and the small settlement in New Orleans were no worry to the Spaniards who claimed the West all the way to the Pacific Ocean. But two million energetic and ambitious farmers, merchants and frontiersmen along the Atlantic Coast were definitely a threat. Spanish authorities in Mexico, joining forces with missionary leaders, moved north into California nearly two hundred years after Columbus had landed on the islands of the Caribbean. In 1769, the same year that Daniel Boone looked down from a high point onto Kentucky, the Spanish explorer Portola breasted a rise in California and became the first European to gaze upon the great bay at San Francisco.

Later that year, the first herd of cattle was brought in from Mexico and, two years later, wheat was sown near the San Diego Mission. Thus was begun the establishment of the famous twenty-one Spanish Missions, extending northward some 500 miles along the coast to San Francisco. The padres, under the leadership of Fray Junípero Serra, found a soil and climate similar to their native Spain and with intelligent planning and careful management, and the use of crude tools, irrigation and the labor of docile coastal Indians who readily submitted to strict authority, they created a thriving livestock industry and propagated a great variety of fruits, nuts, and vegetables. The orchards and gardens of the twenty-one missions never totaled more than 700 acres, but oranges, lemons, apples, grapes, cherries, dates, plums, pomegranates, walnuts, olives, and figs were marvels to travelers, many of whom had existed for months on the coarse and monotonous fare of the trail or long sea voyage.

It is curious that California, which has become first among all states in the sale of farm products, got its agricultural start with a group in which neither management nor labor knew much about farming.

Photo: National Archives

74

Raising the Liberty Pole, 1776

A feeling of freedom of action and a disregard for the opinions and wishes of the mother country, some three thousand miles away across a stormy sea, had prevailed among the English colonists since early days. This spirit of independence increased when the threat of Spanish domination was dissipated through the efforts of the British sea dogs and the successful attempt of Oglethorpe to set up Georgia (1733) as a buffer between the English colonists and the Spanish in Florida. The feeling of self-reliance and independence received another boost at the end of the Seven Years' War, or French and Indian War (1763), when the French gave up their ring of forts around the frontier, thus removing another threat to the colonists. The attitude of most colonists was that they were simply Englishmen overseas, entitled to all the rights and privileges of those at home in the British Isles. They were neither "colonial natives," "foreigners," nor "Britishers, second class"; they were loyal members of the Empire helping to make it great and they should be so treated.

If any one thing can be said to have brought on the Revolution, it was the Stamp Act, passed by Parliament in 1765. According to the Act, an official British tax stamp was to be placed on legal papers, newspapers, and practically all published material in the colonies. Although the cost of the stamps was small, they affected every colonist, up and down the coast, and from seashore to backwoods frontier, regardless of social position or type of occupation, and resentment quickly reached major proportions. The Stamp Act convinced many Americans that the only way they could secure their rights as freeborn Englishmen and avoid a steady decline into economic, social, and political slavery was to resist forcibly the crown. By 1776 dissatisfaction with colonial rule and especially the actions of King George III crystallized opinion, and the colonies took up arms against the most liberal government then in existence. Support for the independence movement came from all levels of society and for a variety of reasons. Small farmers resented the British Proclamation of 1763, designed to reduce Indian trouble, which prohibited migration beyond the mountains. Townspeople wanted greater freedom in handling local affairs and they objected to a paternalistic "foreign" government. Shopkeepers and traders abhorred British taxes and any restraint on trade, especially on lucrative New England commerce with the West Indies. Southern planters were weary of being compelled to trade only with England at its prices, terms, and conditions. Although most factions at the outset desired merely to "show England a thing or two," the rising tide of independence soon developed into a drive for a complete break with the mother country.

Print: Library of Congress

The Minutemen of the Revolution

At the outbreak of hostilities the colonies naturally had no unified army, only a few poorly trained and scantily equipped militia. However, in those days practically all men and boys learned to handle firearms and to shoot straight at an early age, and every home had its British-made musket hanging over the fireplace. It was this that strengthened the will and enhanced prospects for independence, for in all history despots had never long prevailed when the ordinary man had in his hands weapons equal to those of the ruling class. The right of every man to possess personal weapons was considered so important that later when the second amendment to the Constitution was written it stipulated that "the right of the people to keep and bear arms shall not be infringed."

Here in dramatic fashion is depicted the basic military policy of the United States since colonial days. From the beginning the American people have feared that a large standing army would eventually destroy their freedom, lead them into needless wars, and set up dictatorships of the European type from which many emigrants had fled. As a consequence, the idea has been firmly held that a small army, or none, was best, and that if danger arose every man should grab his rifle, rush to the defense of his home, and make

short work of the invader. During the Revolutionary War such citizen soldiers were called "minutemen" on the assumption that if needed they would be ready at a minute's notice.

The fear of militarism continues strong, although Americans are admirers of individual war heroes and have elected many of them to high office, including the Presidency. There seems to be a distinction, however, between the professional military man and the "civilian in uniform." For example, Washington, Jackson, the Harrisons, Taylor, Grant, Hayes, Theodore Roosevelt, and Eisenhower all had outstanding war records which helped put them in the White House, but only Grant and Eisenhower were West Point graduates and had made the military their career. It should be further noted that following World War I General "Black Jack" Pershing, the ideal of professional soldiers, was denied presidential nomination. After World War II another famous officer, General MacArthur, was passed over in favor of a man with an equally brilliant war record, one who had the wide grin and friendly manner generally associated with the farmer or merchant who, when trouble came, signed up for the duration of the conflict.

Print: Library of Congress

Washington and Lafayette Visit Soldiers at Valley Forge

Perhaps the darkest hours of the War for Independence occurred during the miserable winter of 1777–78 when Washington's army of a few thousand ragged, hungry, sickness-weakened troops huddled in the bitter cold at Valley Forge, Pennsylvania, and kept the British forces in Philadelphia under observation. Any who think that American liberty was easily won should look to Valley Forge. There in the bloodstained snow an army was molded from untrained, homesick boys drilled and drilled again under Steuben, veteran of Frederick the Great's Prussian army; the Polish patriot, Kosciusko; the young Frenchman, Lafayette; and American officers. The young soldiers needed only the discipline of rigid training to weld them into a cohesive army. Fortunately, in actual combat, the European close-order attack and indiscriminate mass firing was abandoned. Instead the colonials took cover behind trees and rocks and, firing with deadly accuracy, picked off the enemy individually.

Print: U.S. George Washington Bicentennial Commission

General Marion at His Swamp Encampment
Invites a British Officer to Dinner

Although most of the better known incidents and battles of the Revolutionary War took place in Virginia and farther north, the deep South fully supported the War for Independence and numerous engagements took place in the Carolinas and Georgia. General Francis Marion, a South Carolina Huguenot, using frontiersmen mounted on swift horses, kept much larger British forces immobilized by his "hit and run" surprise attacks. On one occasion General Marion, called the "Swamp Fox" by his opponents,

received a British officer under a flag of truce at his wilderness headquarters, which was simply a clearing in the woods where the only seat was a fallen log, the dishes were pieces of bark, and the meal a few sweet potatoes baked at an open fire. The Englishman, amazed and impressed by the cheerful and enthusiastic way Marion and his men accepted the hardships and privations of war, said upon returning to his headquarters that it was useless to fight such people. The tactics of Marion and other Southern leaders were so effective that at the end of the war only Charleston and Savannah were in enemy hands.

Print: Library of Congress

General George Rogers Clark Holds the West

Beyond the mountains the war was a bloody contest between the scattered frontier settlements and the British, the latter coupled with Indian allies who could not always be restrained to conventional standards of warfare. The desperate plight of the pioneers aroused the fury of George Rogers Clark, an aggressive young Kentucky officer, who in 1778 gathered a band of about two hundred veteran frontiersmen and by surprise attacks captured Kaskaskia and Cahokia, on the Mississippi River near St. Louis, and Vincennes, Indiana, on the banks of the Wabash River. These successes at first seemed to assure reasonable safety for settlers in the Old Northwest, and emigrants began to pour into the region. However, renewed Indian attacks made possible by the refusal of frontiersmen to carry on a sustained effort against far distant foes ended the westward movement until the War for Independence was finally won. Most of the Indians, impressed by generous gifts, sided with the British, a decision they were to regret later when the colonists, having gained their independence, looked upon them as defeated enemies.

Photo: Vincennes, Ind., Chamber of Commerce

A British Cartoonist Depicts the End of the Revolution

Victory finally came in 1783 when the Treaty of Paris was signed eight years after the embattled farmers at Lexington and Concord "fired the shot heard around the world." The conflict had dragged out interminably because of difficulties the British had in waging a war so far from home and because of a lack of energetic action by some British commanders. On the American side, the war effort had received only partial and intermittent support. About one-third of the colonists remained loyal to the Crown, (called Tories or worse by colonists and "United Empire Loyalists" by the British), another third was indifferent and the remaining third had difficulty maintaining sustained enthusiasm for their cause. Peak strength of the Continental Army totaled 35,000 in November, 1778, but probably at no time were there more than 20,000 effectives. Due to "summer soldiers and sunshine patriots," at times the number dwindled to less than 2,000.

The end of the war brought staggering problems with which the weak Continental Congress, operating under ineffective Articles of Confederation, was poorly equipped to handle. There followed a period of confusion in which the former thirteen colonies strove to learn how to govern themselves individually and collectively and to retain and develop holdings beyond the Alleghenies. The British, French, and Spanish connived with disgruntled frontier leaders in abortive attempts to separate the western territory from their seaboard capitals and kept the Indians stirred up against the tide of emigration which was running increasingly strong.

Photo: Library of Congress

THE HORSE AMERICA, *throwing his Master.*

Pub.ᵈ as the Act directs Aug.ᵗ 1.ˢᵗ 1779 by M.ʳˢ White, Angel Court, Westminster

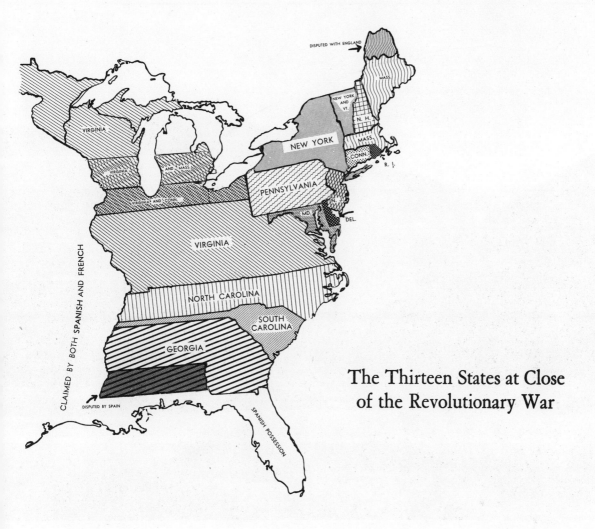

DISPUTED WITH ENGLAND

CLAIMED BY BOTH SPANISH AND FRENCH

DISPUTED BY SPAIN

SPANISH POSSESSION

VIRGINIA

VIRGINIA AND MASS.

VIRGINIA AND CONN.

NEW YORK

PENNSYLVANIA

NEW YORK AND VT.

MASS.

N. H.

CONN.

R. I.

MD.

DEL.

VIRGINIA

NORTH CAROLINA

SOUTH CAROLINA

GEORGIA

The Thirteen States at Close of the Revolutionary War

The land beyond the mountains all the way to the Mississippi River was claimed by individual states along the coast. Mindful of the fact that in their quarrels with England they had always claimed equal status for themselves, goaded by liberal leaders, and compelled by fear of losing the riches to be derived from sale of western lands, the Confederation pushed through the Land Ordinances of 1785 and 1787 which provided for orderly development of the West and eventual equal status with the original thirteen states. These remarkable documents specified that the territory was to be laid off in sections one mile square containing 640 acres, thirty-six sections making up a township. The sixteenth section in each township was to be used to support a public school, the rest of the land to be auctioned to the highest bidder at a minimum price of one dollar per acre. A governor, a sec-

retary, and three judges, all appointed by Congress, were to govern the territory until it had a population of five thousand free males, at which time a representative assembly could be created. When the population of a region reached sixty thousand free inhabitants, it was to be admitted as a state on an equal footing with original states in every respect.

A convention, held in 1787 to revise the Articles of Confederation, produced a completely new Constitution that, with certain amendments, is still in effect. George Washington became the first President under the new Constitution, served two terms (1789-97), refused a third, and returned to Mount Vernon, where he died December 14, 1799. At that time the population was about five million, three hundred thousand, a gain of over five million during the previous one hundred years.

Modern View of Cumberland Gap

The conclusion of the Revolutionary War lifted the restriction placed by England on westward expansion, and, with veterans receiving grants of land for war service and thousands of land-hungry young farmers being dazzled by tales of the lush lands beyond the mountains, the movement west became a surge that blocked the roads and trails leading through the mountains. This westward movement was general all along the Eastern coast, including the lower South, but nowhere was it better dramatized than in Daniel Boone's efforts to move settlers into Kentucky. Cumberland Gap, at the junction of Virginia, Kentucky, and Tennessee, was one of the few gateways through the mountains, and over the years a steady stream of emigrants passed through the gap to follow a rough trail known as the Wilderness Road into Kentucky and on to the Middle West.

Photo: Tennessee Conservation Department

Boonesboro under Indian Attack

At first in order to protect themselves from Indians, settlers huddled together in fortified centers. During Indian attacks, such as here depicted at Boonesboro, Kentucky, women fought alongside their husbands, and children helped mold bullets, put out fires caused by flaming arrows, and cared for the wounded. Gradually, as the Indian menace subsided, pioneers built log cabins on their own land and started clearing the forest.

Colonel Ebenezer Zane, who was part Indian, built Fort Henry, which was saved during an Indian attack by his sister Betty Zane when she ran a gantlet of fire carrying a sack of gunpowder. A descendant, Zane Grey, author of western stories, wrote about this incident in his first historical novel.

Photo: National Archives

Philadelphia—Lancaster Turnpike, 1795

The man of the forests shown standing in the middle of the Lancaster Pike in 1795 could well have been considering the significance of the good new highway, the commodious tavern, the well-filled stagecoach and the covered wagon carrying emigrants west. The country east of the Alleghenies had a population of over four million—more than twelve per square mile —the forests were disappearing, game was getting scarce, and Indians had been subdued. It was clearly no place for a woodsman, but far away on the frontier of the Ohio country was a land where the hunter and trapper could roam the wilderness as of old. A restless, robust young nation was on the march, determined to create a better life for itself and for future generations.

Photo: U.S. Bureau of Public Roads

"Home, Sweet Home," Birthplace of John Howard Payne

The American's love of the home, akin to that of people everywhere, is perhaps best expressed in the sentimental song, "Home, Sweet Home," by John Howard Payne, who was born in this modest dwelling at East Hampton, New York, in 1791. Payne was in Paris far from old familiar scenes when he wrote the nostalgic song that begins " 'Mid pleasures and palaces though we may roam, Be it ever so humble, there's no place like home!"

The home has always been the center of American life. In the early days the girls of the family learned to cook, sew, do housework, and occasionally help in the field. Boys assisted with the regular farm work and such chores as cutting firewood, drawing water, splitting rails, and milking cows. Except in a few very strict groups fun was always an important factor, with young folks engaging in square dances, bobbing for apples, attending picnics, and holding quilting parties, needlework sessions, and husking bees, where the first to find a red ear of corn was thereby marked for early marriage.

On the frontier it was customary, when a young couple got married, for friends and neighbors to hold a "house raising" during which, in a day or two, a one-room log cabin was put up for them. The young bride was expected to have a "hope chest" filled with quilts, needlework, and other useful demonstrations of her handiwork. On occasion a more well-to-do bride brought to the marriage a cow or some other form of dowry. The young man usually had a horse or two, certain essential tools and equipment, and a mortgage on the land which he expected eventually to own.

Customs have changed over the years, but many young people still have household duties to perform and numerous homes have a recreation room set aside for table tennis, dancing, singing around the piano, and games of various sorts.

Photo: William Boone Studios

Primitive Tools Still Being Used at Close of Eighteenth Century

At the close of the New World's third century (1700–1800) most farmers were still using the hand sickle, the flail, the treading floor, and other simple and crude farm implements little changed from Biblical days. An all-iron plow was invented in 1796, but it was only a partial success as the point and cutting edge soon wore off and the expensive plow became useless. These crude implements and unscientific farming methods resulted in wasteful use of land and the depletion of soils all along the Atlantic seacoast and were a factor in promoting westward expansion as young farmers forsook worn-out land and headed across the Alleghenies. By 1800, despite the fact that this nation was still using primitive methods of production, mighty forces were in motion and great changes loomed.

Print: National Archives

Sketch of Eli Whitney's Cotton Gin, 1793

Often, momentous events are hardly noticeable at the time they occur. Such was Eli Whitney's invention of the cotton gin in 1793. At that time cotton production in the entire United States amounted to only 10,000 bales annually, but in six years, because of the new gin, it had skyrocketed to 73,000 bales; in another ten years (by 1810) cotton production was up to 178,000 bales, and it nearly doubled each decade until in 1861 when, at the outbreak of the Civil War, almost 4,500,000 bales were ginned.

Whitney, a Yankee with a mechanical turn of mind, was visiting in the South following his graduation from Yale when he started working on the problem of a cotton gin at which others had struggled without success. In a letter to Thomas Jefferson, Eli Whitney said of his invention: "It is turned by *hand* and requires the strength of one man to keep it in constant motion. It is the stated task of one Negro to clean fifty weight (I mean fifty pounds after it is separated from the seed) of green seed cotton per day." Below is a drawing of a saw-type gin developed after Whitney's original model. Authorities seem to differ whether the saw teeth was Whitney's idea or that of another person.

Jefferson, always on the alert for new and useful ideas, recognized its labor-saving possibilities, but apparently even that farsighted gentleman failed to appreciate the consequences of such a machine. The cotton gin fulfilled the last of the major needs of the textile industry at that time, as the basic machines for spinning, weaving, and carding had long preceded the gin. Thus, by 1800 the stage was set for the fantastic spread of cotton culture on the virgin soils of the South, with its attendant spread of slavery, the plantation system, ruinous farm practices, the rise of a "cotton aristocracy," and the political struggle between North and South which culminated in the Civil War and its awful aftermath.

Print: Smithsonian Institution

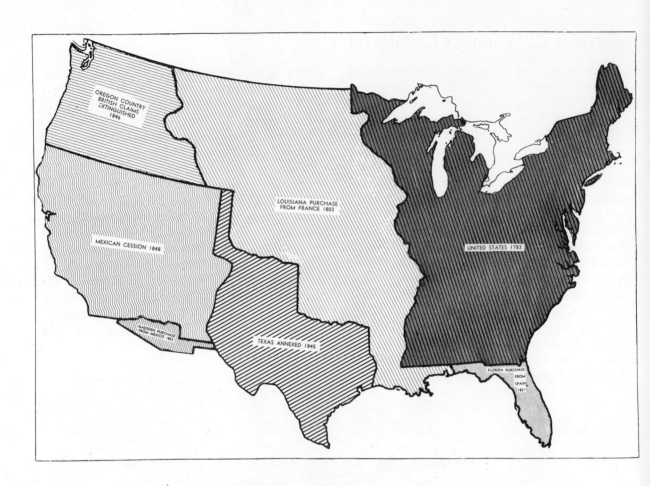

Territorial Acquisitions
1783–1853

VI. THE FOURTH HUNDRED YEARS—1800-1900

EXPLORERS, TRADERS AND TRAPPERS—GROW-
ING WEST TO THE MISSOURI RIVER—THE FAR
WEST BEYOND THE BIG MUDDY — AMERICA'S
TRAGIC CIVIL WAR—THE LAST WEST—LEAVEN-
ING THE LOAF—FROM FARM TO FACTORY—THE
LONG BEGINNING ENDS—INDUSTRY TAKES OVER

In 1800 a robust young nation, after 200 years of in-
cubation along the Coast, had finally cracked its shell
and started out on its own. The small farmers, shopkeepers, and mechanics had had enough of the colonial way of life and were determined to create something better in the fertile lands beyond the Alleghenies. The people were on the march and nothing could
stop them. Nothing, nothing at all, could withstand
the terrific power of a determined man with his family, plow, and cow. Hardships and dangers were the
daily companions of the pioneers pushing ever westward and many and bitter were the personal tragedies
occurring along the way, but the survivors closed
ranks and the march continued.

As the pioneers saw it, the Indians not only had
done little to improve the area during their tenancy
of several thousand years, but had sided with the British in the Revolution; hence they, too, had lost the
area to the victorious colonists. The French had a
whole century to do something with the Mississippi
Valley before losing it to England (in the Seven Years'
War), but had accomplished little beyond exploiting
the fur trade. The Spanish claimed the country beyond the Mississippi River in which they maintained
a few outposts, but what had they done during 200

years to establish a higher claim than a man who
wanted to build a home, raise a family, grow crops,
and bring the blessings of civilization to the backwoods? No, the pioneers, many of them veterans of
the War of Independence, were in no mood to tem-
porize—they were going to make a great country out
of this wilderness regardless of obstacles, and anyone
who got in the way of this objective was going to be
in trouble.

Opening of the Ohio territory to settlement beck-
oned to the land-hungry throngs from Maine to
Georgia and they took off across the mountains in a
tumultuous surge that in 50 years carried them across
3000 miles of trackless wilderness to the shores of the
far Pacific.

The march had barely gotten under way when
President Thomas Jefferson made the Louisiana Purchase, which doubled the size of the infant nation,
assured use of the Mississippi River and stirred up another wave of pioneers heading for the West. The
Napoleonic Wars finally involved the United States
just as European Wars before and since have done.
Irritation with both the British and French over in-
terference with our commerce, and worry of the Mississippi Valley settlers over an outlet for their produce

through New Orleans finally resulted in the young "War-Hawks of the West" obtaining action against England in what we call the War of 1812.

Spain's colonies in Central and South America gained their independence, the United States bought Florida, and tried unsuccessfully to buy Texas from the New Republic of Mexico. Texas broke away from Mexico and set itself up as a Republic but after nine years it joined the United States. This action precipitated war with Mexico (1846), ending two years later with the United States keeping Texas and getting California, Nevada, and Utah and portions of Colorado, New Mexico, and Arizona in exchange for $15,000,000. Meanwhile Britain and the United States agreed upon a northern line for the Oregon Territory and this essentially completed the present boundaries of continental United States. At this moment the discovery of gold in California launched a wild rush of people to the gold fields as others followed the Oregon Trail to the new farm lands in the Pacific Northwest. Westward expansion was the most important single factor of the 19th century, affecting all phases of our political, economic and social life and largely making us what we are. The purchase of Alaska from Russia in 1867 and the acquisition later of Hawaii, Puerto Rico, and other out-lying areas were not a significant factor in the westward movement.

As these stirring events were transforming the West, the vigorous rattle and bang of the embryo industrial revolution had fallen on the receptive ears of the energetic, intelligent, ambitious craftsmen of northern towns and villages who much preferred factory life to that of the frontier farmer. Meanwhile cotton and slavery were spreading across the South as a free soil, family size farm economy was developing in the North and the question of whether new States coming into the Union would be "slave" or "free" was becoming increasingly acute. Various compromises delayed a resort to arms, but finally Civil War came

in 1861, and when it ended four years later, slavery was abolished, the Union was preserved, and, although the South was prostrate, the rest of the country was bursting with energy and anxious to push ahead. The railroads spanned the Continent and branched out in all directions to provide the long-haul transportation so essential to the development of the West.

Immigration reached new heights in response to the lure of land and industrial opportunities. Scarcity of labor which had fostered slavery in the South, large families in the North, a disdain for servants in the West, and a general high level of wages, now added impetus to the invention of labor-saving machinery and the development of efficient production, handling and processing methods.

The sailing ship reached its zenith and then was replaced by the mighty steamboat. The telegraph and cable solved the age-old problem of quick communication between distant points across land and sea. The spread of general education, from elementary school to college, to all classes of society unleashed manifold talents formerly left to wither and die. Shortening of the workweek gave the masses of people a degree of leisure never previously enjoyed and they responded with characteristic energy by developing outdoor sports and athletic games of every sort.

In one short century the youthful nation spanned a continent from coast to coast, increasing its population from 5 million to over 70 million, and in the process forests disappeared, frontier outposts became towns, towns became cities, the wilderness became a fenced pasture, the wild Indian a tame sheepherder, and a household enterprise a giant industrial corporation. From 1800 to 1860 expansion to the West was the prime activity. From 1860 to 1900 unification, consolidation and development, especially of the industrial economy, were the major concerns.

Monticello, Home of Thomas Jefferson

Visitors from abroad are sometimes uncertain why there is a national monument to Jefferson in the nation's capital comparable to those for Washington and Lincoln. The reasons are many, but perhaps it is chiefly because Jefferson by word and deed personified the spirit of liberty and the dignity of the individual. He said, "I have sworn upon the altar of God eternal hostility against every form of tyranny over the mind of man." He put this philosophy into action in the Virginia Statute for Religious Freedom. On Jefferson's seal ring was engraved "Rebellion to tyrants is obedience to God." Jefferson implemented this motto when he literally risked his life as well as his property as a leader of the American Revolution. As author of the Declaration of Independence he wrote, ". . . all men are created equal—endowed by their Creator with certain unalienable rights . . . life, liberty and the pursuit of happiness." He freed his own slaves, and he proposed that after 1800 slavery be forbidden in any national territory, but this was defeated by the margin of a single vote.

Monticello, meaning "Little Mountain," the home of Thomas Jefferson, was a fine mansion designed by him and finished to perfection over a period of many years. Jefferson adapted the architecture of ancient Greece to the American scene, thereby setting a style of columned houses which spread throughout the South.

The interests and accomplishments of Jefferson were many and varied. He was a systematic and skillful farmer, and he invented many useful things, including a dumb-waiter and a folding ladder. He was an accomplished violinist and a patron of the arts; he was largely responsible for the writing of the Declaration of Independence; he executed the Louisiana Purchase; he founded the University of Virginia; he designed and drew the plans for numerous great houses as well as the University of Virginia; he was Governor of Virginia, Secretary of State, and President; he wrote the Virginia Statute for Religious Freedom; and he compiled his own Bible, including forty-six pages of the words of Jesus extracted from the New Testament.

Photo: USDA by Ackerman

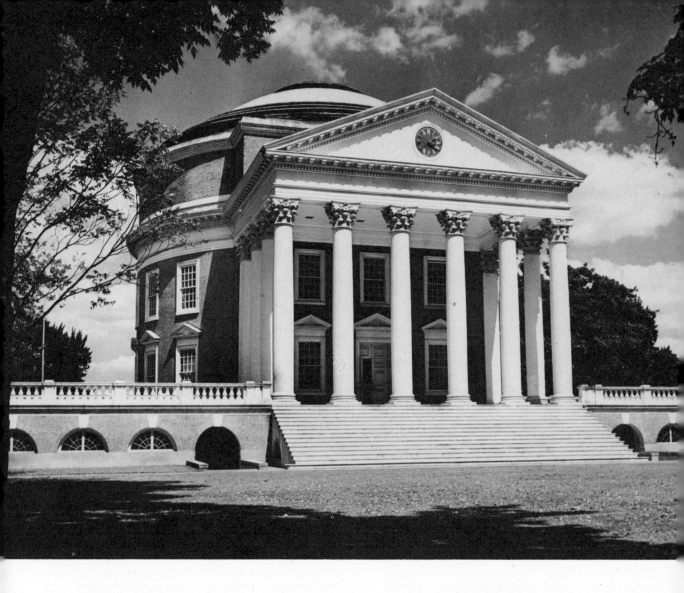

Rotunda at the University of Virginia

Thomas Jefferson believed in the "aristocracy of talents" and promoted development of opportunities for those endowed with unusual ability. He considered the founding of the University of Virginia one of three of his accomplishments worthy of mention on his tombstone. The Rotunda at the University of Virginia sits proudly at the head of the central campus, flanked by columned buildings. Thomas Jefferson, through his field glasses, kept tab on construction of his beloved university from his mountain home two miles away.

The founding fathers apparently did not envision political parties, and during Washington's administration there were none. However, two members of Washington's cabinet, Alexander Hamilton, who favored a strong central government, and Jefferson, who took the contrary view, founded respectively the Federalist Party and the Republican Party (the latter presently called the Democratic Party).

Photo: Ralph Thompson, Charlottesville, Va.

New Orleans

When France gave up its American empire in 1763, there were only a few thousand French in the area compared with a population of over one and a half million in the English colonies. In making peace terms, the French drew the boundary line along the Iberville River rather than the lower Mississippi, thus giving the city of New Orleans to Spain instead of England. Under the Spanish, this seaport developed a colorful population which engaged in trade with Spain, carried on illicit traffic with settlers of the upper valley, and participated in various activities in the Caribbean Sea. When Napoleon conquered Spain he regained the Louisiana Territory, but soon after, eying the rampaging westward expansion of the Yankees, he sold to the United States (1803) not only New Orleans but the five hundred million acres of land funneling north and west all the way to the Rockies and the Canadian border. Napoleon justified his sale of the Louisiana Territory on the grounds that France needed the fifteen million dollars, and besides, he said, the Americans were going to take the land anyway.

Photo: Bureau of New Orleans News

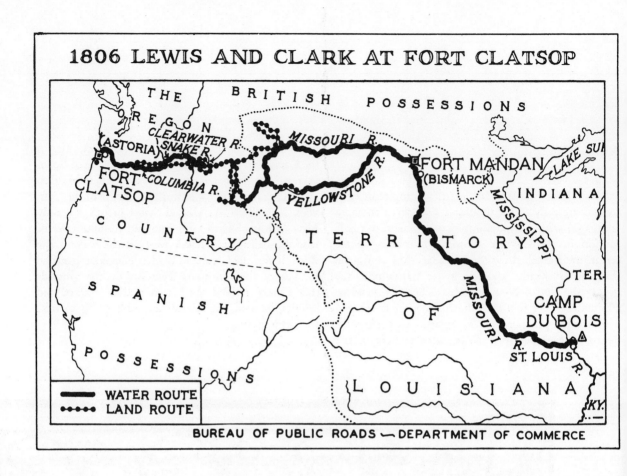

1806 LEWIS AND CLARK AT FORT CLATSOP

BUREAU OF PUBLIC ROADS — DEPARTMENT OF COMMERCE

Lewis and Clark Explore the West

Long before the Louisiana Purchase Thomas Jefferson was considering means by which the territory beyond the Missouri River could be explored without creating trouble with France and Spain. He even undertook to send an ex-missionary and explorer named John Ledyard across the Atlantic to Moscow, hence across Russia and Siberia to Alaska, then down to Oregon where supplies would be secured for an overland trip eastward across the Rockies to the Missouri River. Catherine the Great ended this project by ordering Ledyard out of Russia via Europe. With acquisition of the territory from Napoleon such a roundabout maneuver was unnecessary and President Jefferson commissioned Captain Meriwether Lewis and Captain William Clark to lead an expedition up the Missouri River to its source, overland to the Columbia River, and down to the Pacific Ocean. The explorers returned by approximately the same route, having in two years traveled several thousand miles through a wilderness infested by wild animals and savage Indians. Exposed to severe hardships, illness, and disease, they suffered the loss of only one man, who died of sickness. This first overland trip by white men was aided by a young Shoshone Indian woman named Sacojawea (Bird Woman), who helped guide Lewis and Clark to the home of her people. The expedition brought back a great deal of information concerning the area traversed but several decades were to pass before the people of the young Republic were to know much about their immense new domain. When the dispute over the Oregon Territory was being settled nearly a half century after the Lewis and Clark Expedition that eventful trip played its part in establishing the U.S. claim.

In this painting by Charlie Russell, the giant Negro, York, member of the Lewis and Clark Expedition, is pinched by friendly Mandan Indians to determine whether his color is genuine.

Print: Montana State Historical Museum

Fur Traders on the Missouri Attacked by Indians

As Lewis and Clark were returning from their epochal trip, they met two fur traders far up the Missouri River. Soon there was a flourishing trade along the Missouri, but, as this sketch indicates, it was a hazardous undertaking.

Print: W. M. Cary, Harper's Weekly, *1868*

PARSONS.DEL.   AVERY.SC.

Astoria, Oregon, in 1813

The tempting prospect of enormous profits from the fur trade among Indians of the Northwest resulted in numerous efforts by individuals and trading companies to tap this rich area. Success was limited because of the costly travel involved, the hostility of Indians, and the internecine strife between various fur companies. The most ambitious effort was made by the American Fur Company, headed by John Jacob Astor, who in 1810 sent a group of thirty-three traders "around the Horn" to the mouth of the Columbia River, where they were joined by an overland group of sixty-two men and an Indian woman. The plan was to send a supply ship annually from New York to Astoria which would pick up the furs accumulated during the year, take them to China, where they would bring fantastic prices, take on a return cargo of silks, spices, and the like, and return to New York after a two-year voyage. Despite frightful trials and tribulations inherent in such an adventurous enterprise, an auspicious start was accomplished, which, however, was cut short by the outbreak of the War of 1812, when the defenseless trading post and all its facilities was sold to the English-owned Northwest Company. The latter was soon merged with the powerful Hudson's Bay Company under the energetic leadership of Dr. John McLoughlin, "King of Oregon," and dominated the Northwest until men with plows came and wrested the area from both Indians and white traders.

Print: Oregon Historical Society

Jim Bridger, Mountain Man

When American traders were forced out of the Northwest, they shifted their activities to the Rocky Mountain area where, instead of trading directly with the Indians for furs, they met with hunters and trappers who at an annual rendezvous in some wild spot sold their winter take of pelts to buyers from the East. For twenty-five years the mountain area was a happy hunting ground for those who roamed its vast, lonely, and majestic reaches in search of beaver, mink, otter, and other fur-bearing animals. These wilderness wanderers traced rivers, found passes through the mountains, and blazed trails which later were followed by covered-wagon emigrants, gold seekers, and settlers.

The mountain men appeared to be no great threat to the Indians and they got along reasonably well together, with an occasional trapper taking an Indian wife. This hardy breed of men was typified by the famous Jim Bridger, pictured here, who spent most of his life in the wilderness and whose fort in western Wyoming in later years became an important stop on the Oregon Trail and the Overland Route to California.

Photo: Wyoming State Historical Department

THEY THAT GO
DOWN TO THE SEA
IN SHIPS

Whaling in the North Atlantic

Fishing was a major activity of New Englanders from the beginning, and it took on added zest when a stepped-up demand arose for whale oil to be used in improved lamps of the early nineteenth century. Harpooning a whale was, as this Currier and Ives print indicates, a dangerous occupation, but high prices made the risks seem trivial, and every year whaling fleets set out from New Bedford and other New England ports for the North Atlantic.

Print: Library of Congress

Arguing the Point

The right to argue is a hallmark of freedom. From the beginning the people of the U.S.A. have debated issues frankly, openly and, in the main, good-naturedly. On the farm, in the factory, around the stove in a country store, on street corners, in town meetings, and in the press and over the air issues of the day have been threshed out and subjected to the healthful light of open debate. Here a neighbor reads a news item which evokes a strenuous argument from his friend, who ignores his wife's call for dinner and the persistent tug of his little daughter as he drives home his point. In the Ohio country, where this scene takes place, there was much to debate during the early nineteenth century: where should the county seat of government be located? Does the protective tariff rob the farmer? Do we really need better rural schools? Is it fair for private companies to own roads and charge tolls? Does the iron plow really poison the soil? Does working in a factory ruin the health? Should eastern taxes be used for western projects? How big an army do we need? What should be done about the Indians? Are the territories really ready for statehood?

Photo: Courtesy of the Henry Ford Museum, Dearborn, Mich.

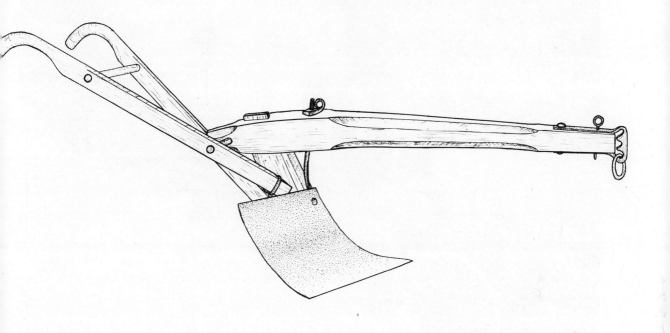

The Plow That Broke the Prairie

Prior to 1814 plows generally were of the wooden type, sometimes reinforced by strips of iron. In that year, however, Jethro Wood invented a cast-iron plow which largely replaced old wooden plows along the Atlantic coastal plain where soils were sandy and loose. When pioneer farmers reached the tall grass prairies of the Middle West they discovered that the iron plows did not work well in the heavy, rich, tough-fibered soil of the prairie. The steel plow was developed which scoured well and was stout enough to withstand the rugged treatment to which it was subjected. This drawing by the Smithsonian Institution is based on the remains of the first steel plow put out by John Deere in 1837. The moldboard and share were cut from a broken steel mill saw and are still in existence. The steel plow was also a necessity on the Great Plains, and together with improved harvesting equipment, threshing machines, and new methods of dry land farming it made crop production possible in the arid West.

Print: Smithsonian Institution

First Steam Railroad in America

Changes were taking place in all phases of the American economy in 1830, but none was of greater significance than the beginning, on December 25, of the first steam passenger service on the South Carolina Railroad (now the Southern). Previous trial runs had been made by the British-built "Stourbridge Lion" on August 8, 1829, and the American-built "Tom Thumb" on August 25, 1830, which the same year temporarily "lost face" by breaking down and losing a race with a horse! However, the train pulled out of Charleston by a locomotive appropriately named "Best Friend" was the real beginning of a transportation system that could haul passengers, mail, and especially heavy freight over the long ground distances that had plagued economic development from earliest days in the Colonies. The coming of the "Iron Horse" marked the end of reliance primarily on water transportation and slow, ponderous wagon traffic. It heralded the day when isolated areas devoid of navigable rivers could be served by fast, efficient, heavy duty transportation. Within five years a thousand miles of railroad track had been laid in eleven states. Within thirty years, at the outbreak of the Civil War, over 30,000 miles of lines were in operation.

Photo: Southern Railway Company

Birthplace of the McCormick Reaper

Inventors worked hard to devise a method of applying horse power to grain harvesting. Success finally came in this small workshop of rough, hand-hewn logs when Cyrus H. McCormick, a Virginia farmer, built the first successful grain reaper in 1831. Recognizing that the center of grain production was moving ever westward and that machine harvesting held greatest promise in the large, level fields of the prairie country, McCormick moved to Chicago in 1847. Four years later he was manufacturing over a thousand reapers each year, whereas he had sold only eighty during the previous decade.

The reaper reduced harvesting costs by one third and was among the first of a long list of labor-saving and efficient farm machines which in time helped one farm worker to produce enough food, fiber, and tobacco for nearly twenty people as compared with only four people in 1840. With the coming of machines to agriculture, the fear of famine disappeared from the American scene. Increased use of machinery moved production from the blacksmith shop to large manufacturing plants and speeded up the development of the factory system. McCormick's wisdom in shifting to Chicago is further indicated by the fact that the center of wheat production moved west more than seven hundred miles to central Iowa between 1850 and 1900, and Chicago became the leader in manufacturing farm machinery.

Photo: by Flournoy

Cradling Grain

The old hand sickle used for harvesting grain since Biblical days was finally replaced about 1800 by the cradle. This implement consisted of a long sharp steel blade and five wooden blades, or fingers, by which, in one sweep, a swath of grain could be cut and piled up for tying into a bundle. Although a great improvement over the sickle, the cradle required tremendous muscular effort.

Photo: USDA by Forsythe

Cotton and Slavery Spread Across the South

In the South cotton was the all-important crop. The market for this product seemed unlimited, and the South wanted more slaves from Africa than shipowners, many of them from New England, could bring to port. Since 1619, when the first slaves had arrived in North America, their numbers had increased as their labor was sought to produce tobacco, rice, indigo, sugar cane, and cotton. The importation of slaves was forbidden by Act of Congress, January 1, 1808. At that time there were 1,191,000 slaves and cotton production amounted to 178,000 bales. Fifty years later, on the eve of the Civil War in 1860, there were about four million slaves and cotton production was up to more than four million bales. During this period of high prices for cotton, most of which was exported to England, a great many cotton planters "mined" the soil, moving on to virgin land further west when it became exhausted.

Photo: USDA

Bound down the River

The Ohio and Mississippi rivers played a major role in the development of the Middle West and especially the South. Flatboats such as the one pictured here were loaded with farm produce and floated down the river, sometimes all the way to New Orleans. The flatboat men were hardened characters and liked to brag of their prowess. A famous riverman known as Mike Fink is claimed to have announced his sentiments in this manner: "I can out-run, out-jump, out-shoot, out-brag, out-drink, an' out-fight—rough an' tumble, no holts barred—any man on both sides of the river to New Orleans an' back ag'in to St. Louie."

In 1811, Nicholas Roosevelt of the Hudson Valley, accompanied by his young wife, made the first steamboat trip down the Ohio and Mississippi to New Orleans, opening a new era which was to revolutionize transportation on western waters. The steamboat, covering eight to ten miles an hour downstream and two miles or better up the river, was vastly superior to the keel boat and other predecessors. Roosevelt's epochal journey was made even more memorable by the New Madrid earthquake, which caused much damage, created Reelfoot Lake, and caused consternation and alarm along the Mississippi. The steamboat on the river and the railway steam engine on land wrought great changes throughout the nation.

Print: Library of Congress

Old Tavern at End of the Natchez Trace

In the days before the steamboat it was relatively easy to float down the Mississippi River, but at New Orleans the flatboat had to be sold, broken up for firewood, or abandoned, and getting back home again was another matter.

A person could come upriver by keel boat, a large rowboat with enough strong men to buck the current. Or, one could walk or ride horseback over the Natchez Trace, which was simply a rough trail running through the forests from Natchez, Mississippi, to Nashville, Tennessee. Since many of the travelers along the Trace carried the profits of their sales in New Orleans, the Trace became noted for its robberies and murders. Meriwether Lewis of Lewis and Clark fame died on the Natchez Trace. This tavern in Natchez was at the end of the long and treacherous Trace.

Photo: National Archives

Plantation House Where Jefferson Davis Was Married

Riding the crest of the cotton boom, some of the newly rich planters built showy mansions while others preferred the lovely "plantation house," such as this one in Mississippi where Jefferson Davis, later President of the Confederacy, was married. The Southern-mansion myth that, prior to the War Between the States, almost every white person down South lived on a big plantation in a large, white-columned, pretentious house surrounded by doting servants is not so much a myth as a gross exaggeration. Throughout the ante-bellum South, where good land, highly valued crops, and adequate transportation, capital, labor, and management converged, there arose spacious and attractive houses where life was lived on a grand scale. All the Southern states had some of these charming places, but clusters of them appeared and can still be seen in the Tidewater tobacco area of Virginia, in Charleston, South Carolina, and nearby in the old rice marshes, among the bayous of Louisiana where sugar cane flourished, along the bluffs of the Mississippi at Natchez where cotton was king, and in the Blue Grass region of Old Kentucky. The notion that all ante-bellum Southerners lived in beautiful mansions is as erroneous as the assumption that all men in the South at that time were tall and handsome, with distinguished-looking mustaches and goatees. The glaring light from crystal chandeliers in the mansions of a relatively few wealthy planters tended to obscure the oil lamps of an infinitely larger number of substantial farmers and overshadowed entirely the glimmer of flickering candles in the homes of small farmers.

Photo: National Archives

Hill Country

As the cotton revolution surged across the rolling hills and coastal plains of the South, life went on much as before in the highlands. Hillsides were cleared and tree trunks split into rails which were used for "snake" fences and the roads were not too bad in dry weather. A small patch of corn and some hay cut from a meadow fed a horse or two, a cow, and a few pigs. Hunting and fishing were good, there were wild berries and fruit to be found, and occasionally one could cut a bee tree for wild honey.

Photo: USDA by Forsythe

Going to Town by Muleback

Going to town on the back of a mule with produce to sell was a standard practice for many generations and still can be seen occasionally in remote sections of the Appalachian Mountains, which extend south to Georgia and Alabama. A trip to the "settlements" on Court Day was long considered a special event.

Photo: USDA by Post

Andrew Jackson, Apostle of Freedom

Andrew Jackson, who rose from poverty and obscurity to wealth and fame in the familiar American pattern, was a typical product of the frontier—energetic, aggressive, and independent. Thomas Jefferson was the founder of the Democratic Party, but Jackson was its flaming spirit. He was a fiercely determined man who did not hesitate to accept the aid of the pirate, Jean Lafitte, in defeating the British at New Orleans in the War of 1812.

It took Jackson thirty days to travel from his home, "The Hermitage," near Nashville, Tennessee, to Washington, D.C., to accept the Presidency. When he died, his old Negro servant, Uncle Alfred, was asked if he thought General Jackson had gone to Heaven. The old man replied, "I don't know whether the General went to Heaven or not, but I am sure that he did if he wanted to!" Jackson stipulated that when Uncle Alfred died he was to be buried near him in the garden of "The Hermitage."

Photo: National Archives

A House Built in Exchange for Two Sheep

During the period of the War of 1812, fantastic speculation arose in connection with Merino sheep imported from Spain. At the height of this speculative frenzy a man in Lexington, Kentucky, agreed to build this house, fifty feet wide and seventy feet deep, in exchange for two Merino sheep. A few months later the bubble burst and the bankrupt builder barbecued his "prize" sheep. The house still stands.

Photo: Lexington Herald-Leader

In 1741, Vitus Bering, a Dane sailing for Russia, discovered Alaska and soon a thriving seal and sea-otter trade was developed and Russian ships were dipping south along the Pacific Coast. Alarmed by these activities, the Spanish in Mexico decided to move north into California and establish presidios and missions. Finally, in 1812, Fort Ross, consisting of a stockade and some sixty buildings, was built north of San Francisco Bay by the Russians, trade was entered into with the presidios and missions, and efforts were made to produce a surplus of crops that could be sent to Russian settlements in Alaska. Destruction of sea-otter herds, mediocre success at farming, the opposition of the Spanish, and the sobering effects of the Monroe Doctrine caused Russia to sell the fort together with thousands of cattle, horses, mules, sheep, tools and weapons to the Swiss settler, Captain John Sutter, and withdraw to Alaska in 1841. The Greek Orthodox Church and a portion of the fourteen-foot stockade shown below are visible evidence that Russia once had a colony in California.

Photo: National Archives

Chapel at Russian Fort in California

Photo: Museum of the Great Plains

Better Roads and Transportation Speed Westward Migration

The Concord stage, above, first made in 1826 in Concord, New Hampshire, was considered deluxe travel, since the upholstered coach, swaying on leather straps, provided a more comfortable ride than had previously been experienced in horse-drawn vehicles. The Concord stagecoach was bitterly resisted by saddle makers and clothiers, who claimed that lolling in a soft-cushioned coach was not only "sissyfied" but actually injurious to health.

In the East it seemed that established towns and villages along the Atlantic coastline would soon be depopulated as family after family headed west to the new frontier beyond the mountains. The persistent demand for better roads finally resulted in the federal government's building the National Road, which by 1818 stretched broad and firm from Baltimore on the Atlantic, to Wheeling, West Virginia, on the Ohio River. Other such roads: Forbes Road connecting Philadelphia with Pittsburgh on the Monongahela River; the Catskill Turnpike, joining the Hudson River with the Susquehanna; and the Genesee Turnpike, linking the Hudson and Lake Erie. These and similar roads built by states and private toll companies aided travel and communication and helped tie the settled East to the pioneer West. A mighty factor in the era of the wagon road was the Conestoga wagon, capable of hauling four tons of freight, depicted below in front of the famous Eagle Inn in Pennsylvania. These sturdy wagons, introduced by the Germans of Pennsylvania, were used by successive waves of pioneers to the Pacific.

Photo: National Archives

Erie Canal Opens New Era of Transportation, 1825

Governor De Witt Clinton of New York, who recognized the potential value of a water route connecting Lake Erie with the Atlantic Ocean, finally on October 26, 1825, after a twenty-year struggle, sat serenely on a gaily decked barge as four horses pulled it along the newly completed canal on a nine-day trip from Buffalo to New York City. Hundreds of cannons, spaced at maximum hearing distance along the route, roared a welcome, and well they might, since the canal was a huge financial success from the start and opened up a whole new region to settlement. About half the wheat exported to Europe passed along the canal and, with transportation charges less than 10 per cent of previous costs, the price of bread for workers of the eastern states and in Europe was greatly lowered. The Erie Canal, in linking the rapidly growing settlements of the Old Northwest to New York, made that city the most important seaport and business center along the Atlantic Coast. The fabulous success of the canal encouraged similar projects designed to tie eastern cities with the booming Ohio country. However, none matched the profitable Erie Canal, and some, such as the Chesapeake and Ohio Canal linking the Washington, D.C., and Baltimore area to the West, were financial failures.

Photo: U.S. Bureau of Public Roads

Clipper Ships Sail the Seven Seas

Shipbuilding was a major enterprise in New England from earliest days, sustained by a steady demand for fishing boats, ships for coastwise trade, and for overseas buyers. The forests of New England provided easily accessible materials, making it possible to build ships much cheaper than in England or on the continent of Europe. But this advantage could not be fully exploited until after the War of Independence. The most spectacular era of shipbuilding occurred from 1840 to 1870 when the famous Clipper ships were built to compete in the highly profitable Far East trade and to speed eager gold-rushers to California. These beautiful, fast, trim ships were adaptations of frigates designed by the French. Below is a painting of the clipper ship *Coeur de Lion* in Hong Kong Harbor in 1854.

Photo: U.S. National Museum

New England Farmhouse and Buildings

The rise of the factory system and the growth of cities provided farmers of the Northeast with a steady and expanding market. As a result farmers increased specialization of farming operations. Dairying, especially the making of cheese, became an important source of income, and hay crops found a ready sale in New York and other cities as feed for dray, carriage, and cab horses. As farmers prospered they built sturdy, compact, attractive homes and outbuildings which frequently were attached to each other so that passage could be made from one to another without one's having to go outdoors during bad weather.

Photo: USDA by Rothstein

Chicago in 1843

It was probably inevitable that the narrow piece of land between the headwaters of the Illinois River and the southern tip of Lake Michigan should become the site of a great city. This small section is tied to the Atlantic coast by the Great Lakes and the St. Lawrence River and is united with the Gulf of Mexico by the Illinois and Mississippi rivers. Marquette and Joliet stopped off briefly in 1673. Little happened during the next one hundred and sixty years, although Fort Dearborn was established in 1803, commanded by Captain John Whistler, whose grandson became a famous painter. Increasing traffic incident to westward migration after 1835 caused the village of Chicago to grow rapidly, and, when this sketch was made, hogs had just been ruled off the streets. Establishment of the McCormick Reaper Company in 1847, the stimulation resulting from hordes of gold-rushers and Oregon Trail emigrants, pulsating steamboat river traffic, the railroad link to the East in 1852, rapid expansion in population throughout the prairie states, and Civil War activities all aided in making Chicago a commercial center. In 1871 disaster struck Chicago when a cow kicked over a lantern, touching off a wind-driven fire which almost destroyed the entire city of three hundred thousand population. Relief funds poured in from around the world and buildings of brick and stone quickly replaced old wooden structures. Cattle from Texas and hogs from Iowa helped make Chicago a meat-packing center. Manufacturing, food processing, transportation, and marketing activities kept Chicago growing, and it has long ranked second only to New York in size and importance among U.S.A. cities.

Print: Library of Congress

The Little Red School House Where Mary Took Her Lamb

New England was a leader in general education. In 1647 Massachusetts passed a law in favor of free schools for all children. The "Little Red School House" supported by public funds, became a symbol in every community of the people's determination to provide educational opportunities for every child. In the classroom and on the playground children of varying national backgrounds, different religions, and from all levels of social and economic strata learned to know and respect each other. A favorite poem, given below, relates an incident that occurred in Sterling, Massachusetts, at the school shown above.

Mary had a little lamb
   Its fleece was white as snow
And everywhere that Mary went
   The lamb was sure to go.

He followed her to school one day;
   That was against the rule;
It made the children laugh and play
   To see a lamb at school.

And so the teacher turned him out;
   But still he lingered near,
And waited patiently about
   Till Mary did appear.

And then he ran to her, and laid
   His head upon her arm
As if he said, "I'm not afraid;
   You'll keep me from all harm."

"What makes the lamb love Mary so?"
   The eager children cry;
"O, Mary loves the lamb, you know,"
   The teacher did reply.

"And you, each gentle animal
   To you, for life may bind,
And make it follow at your call,
   If you are always *kind*."

Photo: National Archives

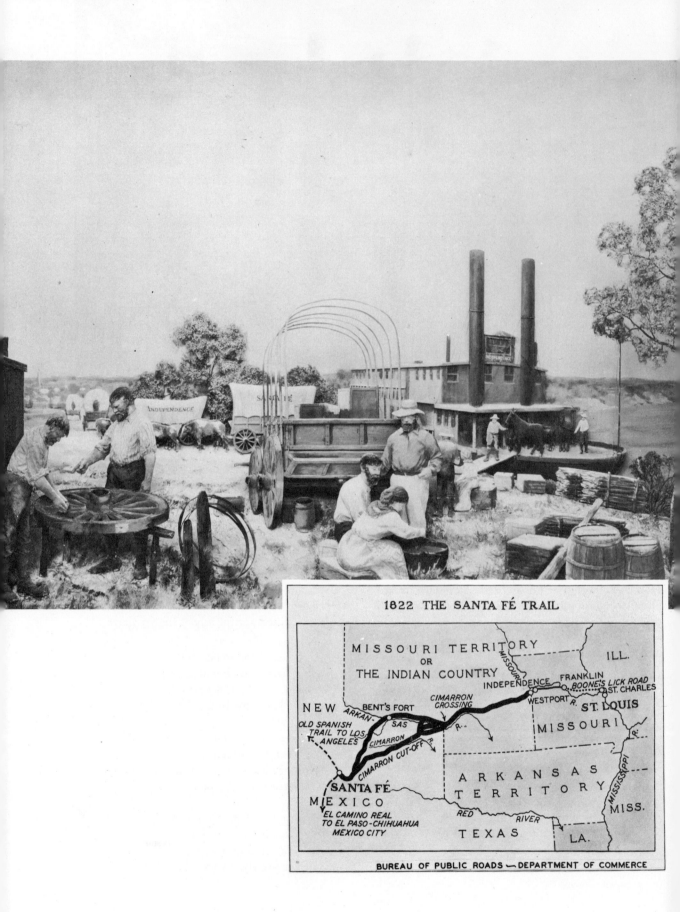

1822 THE SANTA FÉ TRAIL

MISSOURI TERRITORY
OR
THE INDIAN COUNTRY

ILL.

FRANKLIN
INDEPENDENCE
BOONE'S LICK ROAD
ST. CHARLES

NEW
ARKAN-
BENT'S FORT
CIMARRON
CROSSING
WESTPORT
R.
ST. LOUIS

OLD SPANISH
TRAIL TO LOS
ANGELES
SAS
CIMARRON
R.
MISSOURI

CIMARRON CUT-OFF
R.

ARKANSAS
TERRITORY

SANTA FÉ
MEXICO
MISS.

EL CAMINO REAL
TO EL PASO-CHIHUAHUA
MEXICO CITY
RED
RIVER
TEXAS
LA.

BUREAU OF PUBLIC ROADS — DEPARTMENT OF COMMERCE

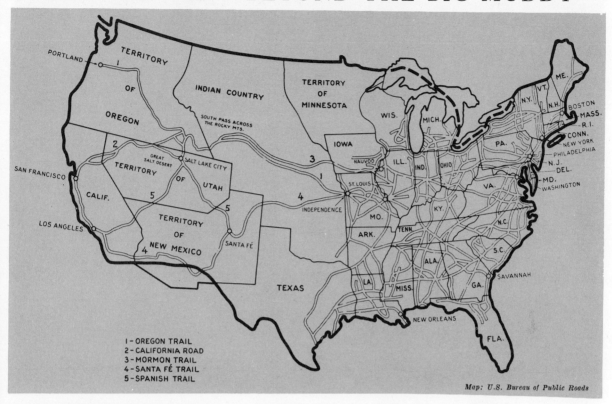

PORTLAND · TERRITORY · OF · OREGON · INDIAN COUNTRY · SOUTH PASS ACROSS THE ROCKY MTS. · TERRITORY OF MINNESOTA · WIS. · MICH. · N.Y. · VT. · ME. · N.H. · BOSTON · MASS. · R.I. · CONN. · NEW YORK · PHILADELPHIA · N.J. · DEL. · MD. · WASHINGTON · PA. · IOWA · NAUVOO · ILL. · IND. · OHIO · VA. · GREAT SALT DESERT · SALT LAKE CITY · TERRITORY OF UTAH · ST.LOUIS · SAN FRANCISCO · CALIF. · INDEPENDENCE · MO. · KY. · N.C. · TERRITORY OF NEW MEXICO · SANTA FÉ · LOS ANGELES · ARK. · TENN. · S.C. · ALA. · GA. · SAVANNAH · TEXAS · LA. · MISS. · NEW ORLEANS · FLA.

1 - OREGON TRAIL
2 - CALIFORNIA ROAD
3 - MORMON TRAIL
4 - SANTA FÉ TRAIL
5 - SPANISH TRAIL

Map: U.S. Bureau of Public Roads

Santa Fe Trail, Trade Route to the Southwest

In 1609, two years after the English established Jamestown, Virginia, the Spanish outpost of Santa Fe was founded as one of several small, mission-type settlements in New Mexico. Two decades later it had a total combined population of a few hundred soldiers, settlers, missionaries, and Indians. Progress was slow, and the struggling community, separated from Mexico City by more than a thousand arid miles and almost impassable mountains, welcomed French traders who, in 1739, established a route across the Plains from the Missouri River. Although trade with the French was officially forbidden by Spanish authorities in Mexico City, traffic continued over the Santa Fe Trail as eastern traders brought in an assortment of manufactured articles which the isolated colonists of New Mexico eagerly purchased with silver, gold, furs, livestock, food supplies, and equipment for the return journey.

Following the Louisiana Purchase in 1803, American traders headed for Santa Fe, which at that time had a population of about two thousand, all anxious for the shop goods of the East. Again, Spanish authorities barred the way. However, when Mexico gained its independence in 1821, Yankee traders were made welcome and the boom era of Old Santa Fe was under way. Indian raiders made travel hazardous, but well-organized and armed convoys of oxen-powered Conestoga freight wagons made annual trips at great profit. Although the volume of traffic was never large and emigrants were relatively few, lessons learned along this old trade route were applied on the Oregon Trail and other pioneer roads of the West.

Photo: National Archives

Mexico Abolishes the Spanish Missions in California

The establishment of the last of the Spanish missions in California in 1823, fifty years after the first one was founded, coincided with the independence of Mexico from Spain, which resulted in the secularization of the missions and their subsequent decline. The ranches and cultivated land of the missions became private property and their gardens grew up in weeds, so that when the United States acquired California in 1848 they had long since lain in ruins. In recent years some of the buildings of the old missions, such as this one at San Juan Capistrano, have been restored. Only the Mission grape, fig, and olive, whose seeds were found in dilapidated adobe walls, exist in California's present-day agriculture.

Photo: National Archives

Sutter's Fort, Headquarters of an Agricultural Empire

During the Spanish period in California there was practically no market outside the area for cattle, and, with most of the better farm land controlled by the missions, efforts to increase the population by bringing in settlers were fruitless. When Mexico gained its independence in 1821, grants of land were made for individual use and for colonization purposes. Land was measured in square leagues (4,438 acres), the maximum for one person being eleven square leagues: one for irrigable land, four for dry-land farming, and six for livestock. Black cattle of Mexico predominated. Only the hides and tallow were marketed by a procedure well described by Dana in *Two Years Before the Mast*. Into this picturesque setting in 1839 strode Captain John A. Sutter, an energetic Swiss, who obtained a grant of forty-nine thousand acres of land along the American and Feather rivers, built a fort on the present site of Sacramento, and enthusiastically set about creating an agricultural empire. Within ten years he was producing thousands of bushels of wheat and other crops and had vast herds of cattle, sheep, and horses. His fort was the center of agricultural expansion for all of central California, and out of a generous nature and desire to promote settlement in the area he had quarters set aside in the fort for weary emigrants arriving by land and sea.

National Archives Sketch by J. W. Revere

Marcus Whitman, Missionary to Northwest Indians

Close behind explorers, hunters, and trappers in the West came missionaries. The most noted of these was Dr. Marcus Whitman, a medical doctor who in 1835 made a trip to the Far Northwest to consider the feasibility of missionary work among the Indians. The next year he returned with his bride and for eleven years they labored to bring the Christian faith to the Indians, heal the sick, carry on agriculture, and encourage and support immigration.

In 1842 "the Good Doctor" again went East to obtain additional aid for his mission and to convince the nation of the vast resources and great importance of Oregon to the future of the United States. On the return trip he provided leadership and guidance for the first wagon train to Oregon. Five years later an epidemic of measles ravaged both Indians and whites, and Dr. Whitman labored hard to save them. A high percentage of Indians died, probably because they practiced an old Indian cure involving a hot steaming bath followed by a jump into the icy waters of a river. The Indians became convinced that the only way to end the plague was to kill the doctor, and on November 29, 1847, he and his family were massacred and the mission destroyed. This statue of Dr. Whitman with his Bible in one hand and medical kit in the other, was placed in the Hall of Fame in the Nation's Capitol by the people of the State of Washington.

Courtesy of the Sculptor, Avard Fairbanks

The Oregon Trail, Emigrant Route to the Far Northwest

The Oregon country, extending from the Rockies to the Pacific Ocean and north from California to Alaska, was claimed by both Great Britain and the United States, with fur traders, missionaries, and settlers from both countries infiltrating the area. Hot-headed Americans used the slogan "54-40 or fight" to indicate their determination to take over the entire area up to the southern border of Alaska. However, the Treaty of 1846 established the boundary of the Oregon territory at the 49th parallel. In the meantime Dr. Whitman's glowing accounts of the wonders of the Northwest appealed to many land-hungry farmers who were anxious both to make a fresh start in new surroundings and to secure the Oregon country for the United States. As a consequence, in the spring of 1843 nearly a thousand men and their families headed west from Missouri for Oregon. Food, clothing, seeds, guns, plows, tools, and other essentials were carried in covered wagons usually drawn by oxen because they withstood the hardships of the trail better than horses or mules and were less likely to be stolen by Indians. The trail led over a tortuous route for more than two thousand miles from Missouri to the Columbia River, where most emigrants put their wagons on rafts to float down the dangerous rapids.

1843 THE OREGON TRAIL

BUREAU OF PUBLIC ROADS — DEPARTMENT OF COMMERCE

Photo: National Archives

Willamette Valley at the End of the Oregon Trail

The end of the trail for many pioneers was the lush and beautiful Willamette Valley in Oregon, abounding in timber, water, and fertile soil, and favored with a mild climate. The valley had the essentials for a great agricultural future, and emigrants from the eastern woodlands recognized its potential from afar and headed their ox teams for it. Most of the thousands who journeyed over the Oregon Trail enjoyed the experience and for the rest of their lives liked to tell of exciting events along the way. Hardships and dangers were ever present, however, and romantic aspects often were quickly changed to sorrow, pain, and disaster. In one wagon train a man suffered a crushed hand which had to be amputated to avoid blood poisoning. There was no doctor or anesthetic available, and all that could be done was to give him a stiff drink of whisky, a fresh chew of tobacco so that he would not grind off his teeth in his agony, to cut off the mangled hand with a hunting knife, and sear the stump with a hot iron.

Photo: Oregon State Highway Commission

John C. Frémont, Pathfinder of the West

Explorations were made by Lieutenant Zebulon M. Pike, who went up the Arkansas River and southward to the Rio Grande River in 1806–07, and by Stephen H. Long, who journeyed west along the Platte River across Nebraska and Colorado to the Rockies and back along the Canadian River during 1819 and 1820. Their reports and those of other sightseers, such as Washington Irving, who saw something of the West in 1833, created much interest but also resulted in much confusion and uncertainty about actual conditions. To help remedy this situation an eager young army lieutenant, John C. Frémont, was sent to explore the Great Unknown west of the Missouri River. During the years 1842–46 Frémont, who was sometimes called "the Pathfinder," made three expeditions to the West Coast in which he established routes used later by emigrants. His enthusiastic reports on the West helped stir the mass migrations that did so much to place western territory under the American flag.

Print: Library of Congress

Kit Carson, the Daniel Boone of the Far West

Frémont's guide on his long exploring trips was Kit Carson, a famous hunter, trapper, Indian fighter, and scout. Carson was of medium height and build, but his courage, skill with a gun, and expertness on the trail won him lasting fame.

Print: National Archives

Joseph Smith, Prophet of the Mormons

Religious persecution has been quite rare in this country, and in its most flagrant instance it led to one of the most dramatic and significant events in the history of the West. In 1820 a young farmer named Joseph Smith, living in a frontier community in western New York, announced that he had received a "heavenly manifestation." During the next several years Smith reported other visitations, and in 1827 he said that the angel Moroni had turned over to him a book with gold pages on which was inscribed in a strange language what purported to be an historical record of a family that had left Jerusalem in 600 B.C. and become the forebears of certain American Indians. The principal chronicler of this record was Mormon, the father of Moroni; therefore, the translation was entitled *the Book of Mormon* and later the members of the faith were nicknamed Mormons.

Joseph Smith understood that he was to establish a church of Christ which was based on the primitive organization, belief in prophecy, revelations, and visions, and which accepted both the Bible and the *Book of Mormon* as inspired scripture. The name chosen for the new movement was the "Church of Jesus Christ of Latter Day Saints." In the early days of the church the Old Testament practice of polygamy was permitted on a restricted basis. Although only about 3 per cent of the church membership ever engaged in the practice, it was seized upon by opponents of the vigorous new faith and caused dissension and strife. The practice was discontinued years later when the United States Supreme Court upheld a law making polygamy illegal.

Photo: L.D.S. Church

Nauvoo, Illinois, Home of Joseph Smith

In 1831 the Mormons left New York because of persecution and began a long bitter search for a haven from the difficulties which drove them from Ohio to Missouri and Illinois, across Iowa and the Great Plains to the Rocky Mountains where they finally found the peace they sought among the "everlasting hills." In 1844 the prophet Joseph Smith left his home in Nauvoo, Illinois and traveled to Carthage to meet with the Governor, but there he was arrested, charged with treason, and murdered by a mob which attacked the jail. A few months later the Mormons began to flee Nauvoo, taking with them only the few belongings that could be carted away.

Photo: L.D.S. Church

Brigham Young, Successor to Joseph Smith

The successor to Joseph Smith was Brigham Young, who proved to be a great organizer, builder, and leader. Several thousand impoverished families headed west for an unknown destination in "the midst of the Rocky Mountains." Along the way they endured the piercing cold of winter and the blasting, dust-laden heat of a long summer trek across the plains. At the end they faced and subdued a barren wilderness unlike anything they had known before.

Photo: L.D.S. Church

The Long Trek West

For the journey west, Brigham Young divided wagons into companies of one hundred with sub-groups of fifty and units of ten with officers in command of each. Young headed an advance contingent of about a hundred and fifty men who scouted the country, located campsites, water, and timber, and occasionally stopped to clear, fence, plow, and plant large sections of ground which later caravans were to harvest. Near the area where Omaha, Nebraska, now stands, a United States Army platoon intercepted Young with a call for Mormon men to serve as volunteers in the Mexican War, then in progress. It was ironical that Mormons were expected to assist a government which previously had disregarded pleas for protection. However, Young saw the wisdom of complying, and five hundred of his youngest and strongest men joined the army. The Mormon Battalion blazed a trail to San Diego, California, by which time the war was ended and they could rejoin their families in Utah.

Print: L.D.S. Church

Salt Lake Valley—"This Is the Place"

As Brigham Young reached the mountains, he watched eagerly for some indication that he had reached the place which years before had been prophesied by Joseph Smith. Finally on July 24, 1847, Young came into view of the Great Salt Lake Valley, at that time a barren, almost flat expanse of desert which had been scorned by the Indians and appeared unlikely to attract anyone else. "This is the place," said Young, and the long search was ended.

Photo: L.D.S. Church

Mormon Temple and Sea Gull Monument

Disaster threatened the pioneers' first year when a plague of crickets attacked the crops. Just as all seemed lost, sea gulls appeared and devoured the crickets. The monument to the sea gulls shown here (foreground) commemorates this event. Gradually, settlements were built throughout the valley and the surrounding areas which today are flourishing communities. Salt Lake City has a population of approximately 200,000, and is reputed to be one of the world's best planned and most beautiful cities. The Temple, in the background, and the Tabernacle, with its mammoth pipe organ, were built during early years in Utah and are indicative of the tremendous energy which transformed a band of harried people into a world-wide organization with over a million members.

Photo: L.D.S. Church

130

The Alamo–A Texas Shrine

The Alamo is sacred to the memory of Davy Crockett, James Bowie, and 180 other brave men who lost their lives there during the War for Texas Independence. In 1821, three hundred years after Cortez conquered Mexico, that country gained its independence from Spain, and the new republic encouraged Americans to settle in the part of Mexico which is now the State of Texas. Differences soon arose between Mexico and its new tenants. Fifteen years later the Texans, under the leadership of Sam Houston, declared their independence and set up a republic which later requested annexation to the United States. After nine years, "Big Foot" Texas, a broad flat land, home of mighty deeds and fabulous tales, joined the Union. The new acquisition was not entirely welcome as northerners were reluctant to see another slave state added. Many Americans groaned at the costs involved, saying that "Texas was just another way of spelling taxes."

Photo: Texas Highway Dept.

Head of Auburn ravine California In the early 50's

California Gold Rush, 1849

James A. Marshall, one of the foremen at Sutter's Fort in 1848, was supervising the construction of a mill on the American River in California when he was attracted by a strange metallic substance in the sands of the river which Sutter quickly identified as gold. Efforts to keep the discovery a secret proved futile and shortly the greatest gold rush of all time was under way. Farmers, lawyers, doctors, sailors, soldiers, the butcher, baker and candlestick maker left their homes in the East and by any means available headed for California. Most of the Argonauts went overland on horseback, by wagon team, and on foot, but many sailed "round the Horn," i.e., around South America. Others took ship to Central America where they crossed the narrow Isthmus of Panama to take ship again for San Francisco. The lure of gold attracted adventurers from all over the world. In the photograph above are a few of the thousands, including Chinese, who came to dig for gold.

Photo: Wells Fargo Bank History Room, San Francisco

"Sunday Morning in the Mines"

The gold-mad men who descended upon Sutter stole his horses, killed his cattle, destroyed his crops, wrecked his buildings, tore down his fences, and brushed aside his claims to the mining property. Instead of becoming rich from the gold discovery, Sutter lost all that he had painfully built up over the years and finally went east to Pennsylvania, where he lived out his days in comfortable but reduced circumstances. When the gold fever subsided, many "Forty-Niners" returned home. Others stayed on and helped to create a great state. This realistic painting by Charles Nahl, who was himself a California gold miner in 1851, depicts activities at a mining camp on a Sunday morning.

Photo: E. B. Crocker Art Gallery, Sacramento

"All That Glitters Is Not Gold"

In the lawless days of the West, finding a secure place to deposit valuables was difficult indeed. In one mining town a bank had a powerful-looking safe, bristling with iron knobs, in which miners confidently placed their gold diggings, convinced that no burglar could crack such a strongly built, sturdy repository. In later years the bank acquired a vault and the old strongbox was placed outside as a memento of Gold Rush days. The rain and sun eventually exposed the old safe as a fake, nothing more than a wooden box covered with sheet iron and flimsy knobs tacked to the sides with two-inch nails. Any safecracker with a screwdriver could easily have ripped the box apart in a few minutes.

In 1852 Wells, Fargo & Company was formed to do a banking, collection, and remittance business in California, the Atlantic Coast States, and Europe. This famous company, which transported millions of dollars of gold and other valuables within lawless areas, put its reliance in strongboxes guarded by heavily armed, courageous, and straight-shooting guards. Bret Harte, who served as a Wells, Fargo "shotgun messenger" during Gold Rush days, later gained fame as the author of "The Luck of Roaring Camp," "The Outcasts of Poker Flat" and other stories of mining camps. The Overland Stage Coach line operated by the Wells, Fargo company required about three weeks to make the two-thousand-mile trip from Missouri to California with its load of passengers, mail, and express.

Photo: Sutter's Fort Museum, Sacramento

Ellis Island, in the "Land of Promise"

As momentous and exciting events were taking place in the West, the North was seeing a rapid natural growth in population, augmented by a tide of immigration unlike anything previously experienced. During the first two hundred years more than 75 per cent of the population originated in Great Britain and Northern Ireland, 8 per cent in Germany, and the remainder primarily in the Netherlands, Sweden, France, and Spain. Germans settled in middle Pennsylvania, where they were erroneously referred to as "Dutch." Scotch-Irish, also misnamed, since they were actually Scotch Lowlanders who had sojourned awhile in Northern Ireland, moved on beyond to the frontier, where they contributed much to the taming of the wilderness.

In early years only the most rugged were able to withstand the hardships of weeks aboard crowded, filthy, disease-infested ships and the terrible plagues, including smallpox and cholera, to which they were subjected on the tempestuous trip across the sea. Official records of immigration begin with 1820 when some five thousand persons were arriving each year. The ebb and flow of immigration varied with the intensity of the "pull" of opportunity in America and the "push" of trying times in Europe. The number of arrivals increased rather slowly until the failure of the potato crop in Ireland (1845–47) and political unrest and economic stress in Germany caused an influx of several hundred thousand each year for a decade. Many Germans settled in the Middle West, especially around Cincinnati, Ohio, St. Louis, Missouri, along the Mississippi River in Iowa and Illinois, and in Wisconsin. Practically all of the Irish stayed in the factory towns of New England, New York, and New Jersey, although some went on to the Middle West.

Following the Civil War, the tide of immigration ran high again, with the "pull" of free land and industrial opportunities enticing northern Europeans, especially Scandinavians, who moved into Minnesota and Wisconsin in large numbers to make this area America's dairyland. From 1880 to 1920 an unprecedented industrial boom and improved travel conditions, with steamships replacing sailing vessels, brought in more than twenty-three million emigrants, of whom 90 per cent were from the Continent, with a high proportion from southern Europe.

Most immigrants, arriving with little money and only a few personal belongings, had to take menial jobs until they had accumulated enough wealth to search for better opportunities. In 1870 about 60 per cent of the immigrants were males, of whom two thirds were between fifteen and forty years of age.

Photo: Corcoran Gallery of Art

Birthplace of Author of McGuffey Readers

Millions of immigrants as well as other Americans were aided in their education by a series of books by William Holmes McGuffey, who was born in this tiny log cabin in 1800. The first of his six *Eclectic Readers* and a high-school reader were published in 1836. Over the years, more than 122,000,000 copies have been sold making the McGuffey textbooks second only to the Bible among best sellers of the world.

Photo: The Henry Ford Museum, Dearborn, Mich.

A Page of a McGuffey *Eclectic Reader*

Lesson XXVII of the McGuffey *Second Reader* is typical of the series and was intended to accomplish several purposes. There were words to learn to spell, an interesting little story that carried a moral lesson, and a number of "exercises" designed to implant the story firmly in the minds of young students, impress on them the moral principles involved, and force them to think about the problems presented.

Photo: U.S.D.A.

60   NEW SECOND READER.

LESSON XXVII.

first	large	could	e'qual	old'er
half	great	woods	a-gree'	call'ed
soon	there	whose	a-bout'	kern'el
once	found	should	be-gan'	quar'rel
shell	broke	un'der	be-longs'	set'tle
John	James	pick'ed	laugh'ing	set'tling

THE QUARREL.

1. UNDER a great tree in the woods, two boys found a fine, large nut.

2. As soon as they saw it, they both ran to get the nut.

3. But James got there first, and picked it up.

136

Discovery of Oil in Pennsylvania, 1859

Oil from living plants and animal carcasses has been a useful commodity throughout man's history, with that produced by commingled bodies of long-buried plants and animals oozing to the surface revealing its presence in the earth to ancient peoples. However, consumption of oil was confined primarily to occasional medicinal applications and use in smelly whale-oil lamps until the mid-nineteenth century, when its use for burning became general. In 1859, Edwin L. Drake, at right in the picture, drilled a well near Titusville, Pennsylvania, which struck oil at about seventy feet, yielding twenty barrels a day. Fortunes were quickly made, causing wild excitement and touching off a search for oil deposits which continues today throughout the United States and around the world.

Kerosene soon banished whale-oil lamps and candles from American homes, except as decorative features, and the oil stove became an active competitor of other forms of heating. Research chemists found increasing uses for the liquid, including gasoline, which around 1900, together with the "horseless carriage," revolutionized transportation and created a vast new industry.

Photo: Drake Well Museum

Camel Caravans in the West, 1857

Jefferson Davis, Secretary of War, 1853–57, later President of the Confederacy, inspired by reports that camels could carry loads of 1,000 pounds thirty-five or forty miles a day, imported some seventy-five camels from the Near East. He enthusiastically sponsored their use in an attempt to establish a communication and freight route across the dry and hot Southern plains and the deserts of the Southwest to California, a new state which Davis hoped to tie as closely as possible to the Old South. The first major test was a trip of 1,200 miles from the Gulf coast of Texas to California, during which the camels thrived on cactus, thistles, mesquite and any other foliage available. They traversed precipitous passes with sure-footed ease, swam rivers, carried loads far exceeding those of mules, remained gentle, placid but sometimes stubborn, and convinced the expedition of their usefulness as trail animals. The camels also caused consternation among the Indians, Mexicans and Americans encountered along the way and scared horses and mules, causing many runaways.

Several private efforts were made to import and use camels in the West but with indifferent success primarily because Americans did not understand camels and camels did not understand Americans. The Civil War interrupted the experiment. Railway and wagon roads soon eliminated the need for camels. Some were disposed of to circuses and others were turned loose to wander the wastelands of the West.

Photo by courtesy Bureau of Public Roads USDC

The Pony Express

and the Telegraph Line

Urgent need for a relatively fast means of communication linking the East with California to help hold that state in the Union resulted in the establishment in April, 1860, of the famous and dramatic Pony Express between St. Joseph, Missouri, and Sacramento, California. A rider traveling at top speed and changing horses with hardly a pause at stations every ten miles or so covered a stretch of about sixty miles, then handed the mail pouch over to another rider who sped it on its way. Thus in nine days the 1,980-mile trip was accomplished. The Pony Express service, which had been operated at a financial loss, was discontinued by Wells, Fargo in October, 1861, when the first transcontinental telegraph line was completed.

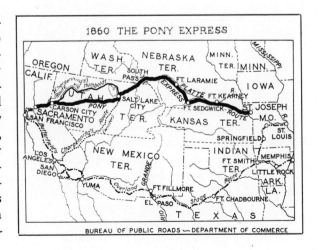

Photo: U.S. Bureau of Public Roads

Photo: Louisville, Ky., Chamber of Commerce

The sun shines bright in my old Kentucky home,
'Tis summer, the darkies are gay;
The corn top's ripe and the meadow's in the bloom,
While the birds make music all the day.
The young folks roll on the little cabin floor,
All merry, all happy and bright;
By'm by hard times comes a knocking at the door,
Then my old Kentucky home, goodnight!

OUR TRAGIC CIVIL WAR

"My Old Kentucky Home"

A young song writer from Pennsylvania named Stephen Foster visited this home (opposite) near Bardstown, Kentucky, and, observing the joys and sorrows of the family, was inspired to write "My Old Kentucky Home," a song that has been a sentimental favorite of the American people everywhere.

After the initial phases of the cotton boom had passed, people of the South went through periods of good and bad times, always attended by the somber problem of slavery. Thoughtful Southerners had long been concerned about the future of an institution which had been outlawed in most parts of the world. There were many aspects to the problem. Was human slavery right? One's conscience had to answer, but could an area be expected voluntarily to give up a 'property" in which it had invested millions? If the slaves were freed, what would be done with them. In many communities they outnumbered the whites. Still, it was generally agreed that slave labor was wasteful and uneconomical. The South indeed "had a bear by the tail and couldn't hold on but didn't dare turn loose."

Moral, social, and economic problems were bad enough, but they were easy compared to the political one which centered around the question of whether new states coming into the Union would be "slave" or "free" states. Upon the answer hung the future political control of the country. If a disproportionate number of states came in "free," slavery would in all probability be abolished, and the South believed it would be ruined financially, socially, and politically. To many Southerners the answer seemed to be secession from the Union. There was nothing in the Constitution which forbade secession, and certain northern states had considered it on previous occasions. Therefore, to many Southerners, horrified at the alternatives, a peaceful withdrawal from the Union and the setting up of a separate republic seemed best.

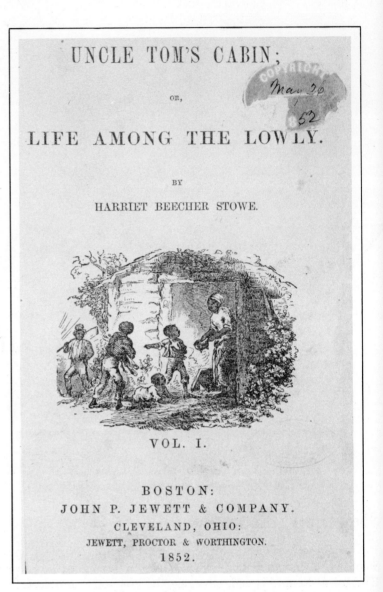

Title Page in First Edition of a Famous Novel

A book called *Uncle Tom's Cabin* so stirred the emotions of the Northern people and made the South so angry that any possibility of a peaceful settlement of the slave question disappeared. Few books if any have played such an important part in a nation's history. Sentiment in the North for the abolition of slavery grew rapidly; smuggling of slaves from the South increased; sympathy grew for John Brown, a fanatic sentenced to death for attempting armed liberation of slaves; and more and more people listened to a tall, homely country lawyer in Illinois, Abraham Lincoln, who solemnly counseled, "A house divided against itself cannot endure. I believe that government cannot endure permanently half slave and half free." Lincoln shortly after was elected President, and South Carolina led the procession of Southern states out of the Union to form the Confederate States of America. On April 12, 1861, guns opened fire on Union forces in Fort Sumter in Charleston Harbor and the Civil War, or the "War Between the States," was under way. The awful conflict became America's greatest tragedy. Slavery was doomed and political ascendancy of the North was inevitable. Had the realistic and less emotional council of men like Sam Houston, Governor of Texas, prevailed, war could possibly have been avoided and desirable objectives accomplished peacefully.

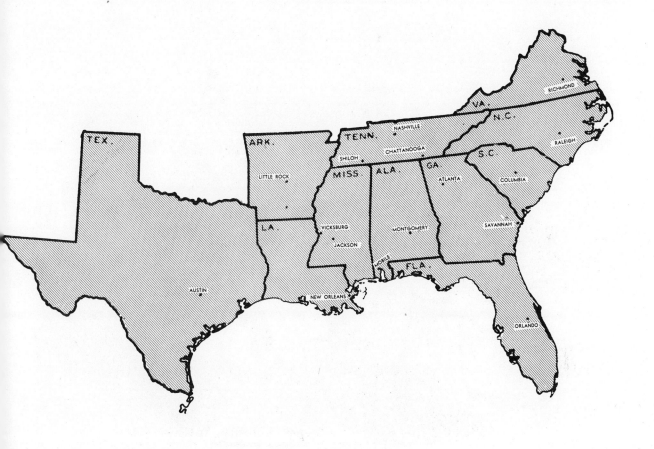

Confederate States
1861–1865

Disunion—North and South

The North and the South were ill matched in population, industrial development, natural resources, transportation, shipping, and credit facilities. The North's population of twenty-two million, four times that of the white population of the South, was steadily augmented by immigration. The North was also superior in the production and maintenance of the sinews of war. The struggle, between an industrial and an agricultural economy, took longer to decide than might be expected, because Southern forces were fighting on home ground with superior military leadership, especially during the early years of the war.

The Confederate government was almost an exact replica of the one from which it had seceded, the home of President Jefferson Davis even being called the "White House." State rights were emphasized, a major factor in the defeat of the South, since state governors often withheld troops, supplies, and equipment instead of submitting all available resources to a unified command. The Confederacy was hampered throughout by a provincial patriotism similar to that which plagued the Continental Congress during the Revolution.

A Struggle Between Southern Cotton, British Textile Mills, and Northern Wheat

With its ports blockaded, the Confederacy desperately needed diplomatic recognition from Great Britain and France in order to dispose of four million bales of cotton piled up at its ports. However, the people of Great Britain were opposed to slavery in principle. Further, although England, with 500,000 people on relief was anxious to obtain cotton for its inactive mills, she also needed wheat from the North to feed her people. The need for bread grains became increasingly imperative because of crop failures in England in 1861, 1862, and 1863, and an adequate supply could not be obtained elsewhere. It has been argued that this need for bread tipped the scales against diplomatic recognition of the South. The McCormick reaper invented by a Virginian helped defeat the South by making possible the harvesting of huge crops of grain on the broad prairies of the Midwest.

France also needed cotton and provisions from the South, and the cartoonist shows Napoleon III, together with John Bull, hopefully sampling Southern molasses. However, France decided against breaking the blockade and turned its attention to Mexico, where Napoleon III set up Prince Maximilian of Austria as ruler.

Print: Library of Congress

Battle of Atlanta, Georgia

During four terrible years the South was a battle-ground as war raged within its borders. Death losses of the Union Army totaled 360,000, of which 221,000 were listed as resulting from disease, 108,000 in battle and 30,000 in war prisons. Authoritative figures concerning Confederate losses are not obtainable, but it seems probable they were about those of the Federal Army. The tragedy was all the more poignant because the issues split communities into bitter factions and pitted friend against friend, brother against brother. During the Battle of Atlanta depicted here, a Union officer rushing forward paused momentarily to give a wounded Confederate soldier a drink of water only to discover that the dying man was his brother. Consider also the anguish of a father like Senator John J. Crittenden, one of whose sons was a general in the Confederate Army and another a general in the Union Army, or the mixed emotions of Colonel J. C. Breckinridge who, during the battle shown in this section of the Atlanta Cyclorama, was captured and made prisoner by his brother, W. C. P. Breckinridge, a "Rebel" in the Confederate Army.

On January 1, 1863, President Lincoln issued the Emancipation Proclamation freeing slaves. In July of that year, the Confederate forces invaded the North and at Gettysburg, Pennsylvania, fought and lost the decisive battle of the war. The South, exhausted by its efforts and the awful destruction of war, staggered on for nearly two more years before collapsing at Appomattox.

Photo: Atlanta Chamber of Commerce

McLean House at Bull Run, Beauregard's Headquarters in First Battle of Civil War

In 1861 Wilmer McLean and his family lived in this house (above) near Manassas, Virginia. The McLeans were a peaceful family, but there was nothing they could do to prevent the first battle of the Civil War being fought on their farm, during which their home was headquarters for General Beauregard. This Confederate commander later wrote, "A comical effect of this artillery fight was the destruction of the dinner of myself and staff by a Federal shell that fell into the fireplace of my headquarters at the McLean House." Wilmer McLean failed to see the humor in this and decided to sell his ill-fated farm and buy another in a part of the state far removed from the scene of battle.

Photo: Library of Congress

McLean House at Appomattox Where Grant and Lee Met After Last Battle of Civil War

The McLeans couldn't escape trouble. Four years later, General Lee and General Grant met in the parlor of Wilmer McLean's home (below) at Appomattox Court House to sign terms ending the War between the States.

Photo: National Archives

Abraham Lincoln

At war's end, with the Union preserved, Lincoln was anxious to achieve the goal stated in his Second Inaugural Address: "With malice toward none, with charity for all, with firmness in the right as God gives us to see the right, let us strive on to finish the work we are in; to bind up the Nation's wounds; to care for him who shall have borne the battle and for his widow, and his orphan . . . to do all which may achieve and cherish a just and lasting peace among ourselves and with all nations." But at his moment of glory Lincoln was shot down by John Wilkes Booth while attending a play at the Ford Theater in Washington, D.C. His plans for sympathetic and generous treatment of the South died with him, replaced by schemes conceived in hate and dedicated to vengeance.

Print: National Archives

"The Lost Cause"

The returning Confederate soldier faced a bleak and seemingly hopeless future. He found his livestock gone, his fields grown up in weeds, his money of no value, his credit weak, and his place in community and state affairs taken over by carpetbaggers from the North teamed up with local "scalawags."

Bitter foes of the South took over Congress following Lincoln's death, installed military government in the South, and passed a Reconstruction Act under which many wrongs were perpetrated. However, the people of this country learned some important lessons from ill-considered reconstruction policies. It became clear that a poverty-stricken South would be not only an unfortunate liability but an open wound which eventually would sicken the entire nation. The theory of the "hard peace" was discredited, and, following the Spanish-American War, people of the United States were determined not to retain the Philippines as colonies but to aid them in becoming a free and independent nation. Likewise, following World Wars I and II, the United States did its best to aid its former enemies to "bind up their wounds" and regain their economic well-being. Had even a modicum of this attitude prevailed after Appomattox, the entire nation would have benefited economically, cordial relations would have been restored sooner, and many problems would have been prevented.

Photo: Kentucky Historical Society

The Evils of War Lingered Long in the South

In 1870, five years after the end of the war, the South's agricultural production was still far below that of 1860. Farm land was reduced 20 per cent, value of farm property 50 per cent, the number of milk cows 22 per cent, other cattle 31 per cent, horses 28 per cent, mules 23 per cent, swine 42 per cent, corn 34 per cent, and cotton production 46 per cent. Not until 1890 did the South begin to get back to prewar levels of production, whereas in the North agricultural output exceeded that of previous years. One-crop farming, poor management, losses resulting from insect pests, soil exhaustion, and difficult economic conditions caused neglect of many old homes which, like this one, were finally abandoned.

Photo: USDA by Postlewaite

The Reign of King Cotton Was Prolonged after the War by the Share-Cropping System

During the war, Negroes in the South conducted themselves well, going about their work, aiding the women left behind by husbands, sons, and brothers in the Confederate Army, even occasionally going along to serve their masters.

When the fever of freedom subsided, the Negro found he had little or no property, scant education, and nothing to work with except a strong back and willing hands. The landowner had a few horses and mules and some broken-down equipment, but not much else. In order for both to survive, each agreed to provide what he could and the crop was divided between them. Thus out of necessity arose the share-cropping system, which was not sound economically and now after three quarters of a century is disappearing. After a period of slow economic progress along with the rest of the war-stricken South, Negroes began to acquire farms and the necessary education and training to begin the most rapid rise economically, socially, and politically of any people in history.

Booker T. Washington

Booker T. Washington, born in Virginia just prior to the Civil War, was graduated from Hampton Institute in 1875. As founder and president of Tuskegee Normal and Industrial Institute, which was established under an act passed in 1881 by the Alabama Legislature, he provided the steadying hand so badly needed by his people at the time. Under his guidance, Tuskegee laid the foundations for its present eminence as one of the largest Negro colleges in the world. In helping to establish harmonious relationships between white and colored and to demonstrate their interdependence, Dr. Washington hammered away on this theme, "You can't keep a man in a ditch unless you are willing to stay in it with him."

Photo: Library of Congress

Early Days at Tuskegee Institute

Tuskegee Institute already had both men and women students when this picture was taken many years ago. Starting with an old church building and a shed, the institute has grown to include nearly four thousand acres of land and 125 buildings. Its Reserve Officers Training Corps turned out hundreds of officers and flyers who served around the globe during World War II.

Photo: Library of Congress

Agricultural School on Wheels

Instruction in new farm techniques and procedures has always been a major objective of Tuskegee Institute. From 1906 until a few years ago, a school on wheels toured the countryside, promoting better farming practices. The truck carried implements and home conveniences of a type the average farm could obtain and use which were demonstrated by a trained worker. Accompanying it also were a woman to demonstrate better home practices and a nurse to give instructions in home sanitation and care of the sick.

Photo: Tuskegee Institute by Battey

Dr. George Washington Carver

Dr. George Washington Carver of Tuskegee gained international fame as a scientist and received many honors for his work. On one occasion he lectured before a group of congressmen for several hours about his research on peanuts, for which he developed more than three hundred uses. The United States has indeed been developed by people of many races, colors, and creeds.

Photo: USDA

The *Natchez* and the *Robert E. Lee* Steamboat Race on the Mississippi River

The steamboat, memorialized by such books as Mark Twain's nostalgic *Life on the Mississippi,* achieved a glamorous and romantic fame unsurpassed by any other means of transportation. The captain of a river packet, a very important and colorful person indeed, stood ready to match the speed of his "floating palace" against that of any other boat on the river.

A highly publicized riverboat race occurred in 1870 between the *Robert E. Lee* and the *Natchez* from New Orleans, Louisiana, to St. Louis, Missouri. As this Currier and Ives print indicates, the *Robert E. Lee* won the 1,200-mile race. The time was three days, eighteen hours, and thirty minutes.

Photo: Library of Congress

"French's New Sensation" Showboat on the Ohio River

"Here comes the showboat!" announced exciting news to townspeople along the river before the turn of the century. It meant that the isolated and hum-drum life of the village was to be enlivened by the presentation of stage plays aboard the boat. Actors and actresses were of moderate talent and the plays were usually melodramas, but to small-town folk starved for entertainment the showboat and its troupe

spelled glamor. The South has always loved the theater and good music, and many favorite songs originated there, such as the beautiful and touching Negro spirituals which are sung wherever Americans gather. More recently "jazz" music, developed along the lower Mississippi and in the night spots of New Orleans, has spread throughout the nation.

Photo: Captain Fred Way, Sewickley, Pa.

Jesse James, the "Robin Hood of the U.S.A."

Jesse James, one of the most controversial characters in American history, is shown here in a picture his wife claimed to be a good likeness. His father, Robert James, was a Baptist preacher when Jesse was born in Missouri in 1847. A boy of fourteen when the Civil War broke out, Jesse soon joined Quantrill's Missouri guerrillas, who fought Union forces occasionally and specialized in robbery and terrorizing the Missouri-Kansas border. His defenders claim that these war-time activities of his youth caused James to pursue a life of crime afterward. There is little doubt that he participated in numerous bank and train robberies. A $10,000 "dead or alive" reward was offered for James, and on April 3, 1882, while standing on a chair dusting a picture in his home, he was shot by a man he considered his friend.

Photo: Montgomery Service, Kansas City, Mo.

Boyhood Home of Mark Twain on the Mississippi

The beloved humorist Samuel Clemens, or "Mark Twain" as he was better known, (1835–1910) lived as a boy in this house in the little river town of Hannibal, Missouri. A modern-day Tom Sawyer and Huck Finn stand in front of this modest home of more than a century ago. At the right can be seen a high board fence such as the one Tom Sawyer enticed his friends into whitewashing.

Photo: Missouri Division Resources and Development

A Church with a Pointing Hand

Probably no other area of the United States has a greater number of church members in relation to its total population than the South. Before the outbreak of the War Between the States, when this church was completed, there were about twenty-one thousand church structures in the South compared with only thirty-three thousand churches in the rest of the country, which had three times as large a population. The unusual church spire with its pointing hand is symbolic of the varied faiths of the people of all the United States. Port Gibson, Mississippi, where the church is located, was spared by General Grant in 1863 because it was "too beautiful to destroy."

Photo: Port Gibson, Miss., Chamber of Commerce

Hear me, my warriors; my heart is sick and sad.
From where the sun now stands I will fight no more
  forever!
       By Chief Joseph of the Nez Perce Tribe

THE LAST WEST

Indian Mode of Traveling

During the Civil War immigration to the Far West slackened, but the coming of peace brought a rush of people determined to subdue Indians and settle the West. The Indians of the Great Plains, mounted on swift ponies descended from horses brought to America three hundred years earlier by Spaniards, were perhaps the most formidable antagonists western pioneers encountered. These nomadic huntsmen were superb horsemen and could shoot twenty arrows with deadly accuracy while the white man was firing one or two shots from his clumsy firearms. Using shield, tomahawk, lance, and bow and arrows, the warrior of the plains was no easy prey even to army dragoons ex-perienced in Indian warfare. The advantage of fighting on home ground was enhanced by a highly de-veloped system of signaling which enabled the Plains Indians to transmit information over vast distances with great speed. Signaling devices included puffs of smoke from a campfire, blanket waving, moving a horse about in prescribed circles and angles, hand signals, and the use of mirrors.

As pictured, the Indian horse was also used to drag a crude platform on poles piled high with household equipment and supplies.

Photo: Architect of the Capitol

Indians and Buffalo on the Great Plains

Bison, or "buffalo" as they were often erroneously called, found in small bands throughout the eastern woodlands by the early colonists, had disappeared east of the Mississippi River by 1832. The real home of these rugged, dull-witted beasts was the Great Plains, where until the 1870's they fed on the short, nutritious grass that then blanketed the area. The hide, flesh, and bone of the buffalo provided the Plains Indian with food, shelter, clothing, implements, and weapons, enabling him to roam over the vast expanse of the treeless plains.

Print: Library of Congress

A Railroad Engine Squirts a Buffalo off the Track

Early estimates of the number of buffalo on the Great Plains ran into the millions, with individual herds stretched out as far as one could see. On various occasions trains were held up for hours, waiting for a large herd to pass. For a time, railroad engines were provided with a water-squirting device used to frighten buffalo off the tracks.

Print: Union Pacific Railroad

End of a Buffalo Chase

Shooting buffalo was a favorite pastime, and railroad passengers occasionally blazed away at them from train windows with no intention of utilizing the hide and carcass of the animals slain. The hunting of buffalo became big business after the Civil War, when hides were in great demand as carriage robes, shoe leather for the East's expanding industrial population, and winter coats for foreign armies. Because of faulty curing methods, probably no more than half of the hides ever reached the markets, while an insignificant number of carcasses were used to feed construction gangs building railroads through the West.

Methods of hunting buffalo varied, but the two most generally followed were by riding into a herd on horseback and shooting the frightened creatures as they ran and by sneaking up on the windward side of a grazing herd and shooting them from a concealed position. It is claimed that on one occasion a hunter using the latter method shot 107 buffaloes in an hour.

Photo: Archives and Western History Department, University of Wyoming Library

Buffalo Hides Ready for Shipment from Dodge City, Kansas, 1874

The magnitude of the slaughter of buffalo is indicated by this pile of hides in Dodge City in 1874, which at that time shipped an average of 1,500 hides per day valued at one to three dollars apiece. In the three years 1872–74, the Atchison, Topeka and Santa Fe railroad alone hauled 459,453 hides out of southwestern Kansas. Within a span of eighteen years (1866–83) some twelve million buffalo were killed, reducing the once enormous herds to a few scattered groups in isolated areas. The destruction of buffalo herds has often been justly criticized, but it did have two important effects. It made easier the task of subduing the fierce Plains Indians who depended upon the buffalo for existence and it made possible the plains livestock industry which would have been hampered in its development so long as buffalo were present in large numbers to compete for the range.

Photo: Kansas State Historical Society

Texas Longhorns, Rugged and Wild Descendants of Colonial Spanish Cattle

The cattle industry in the Western Hemisphere began when seven calves were unloaded from a Spanish ship about 1520. Later, when Coronado made his famous journey northward from Mexico into our Southwest in 1540–42, a number of cattle were taken along, some of which strayed and became the basis for the large herds of wild longhorns that three hundred years later roamed the plains of southern Texas. Such scattered herds had to be handled by men on horseback, and the far-riding Spanish and Mexican ranchers, or "vaqueros," soon created brands to identify their stock.

Also introduced at that time were the cowboy's lariat, chaps (chaparajos), heavy spurs, curb bit, saddle horn, "ten-gallon hats," and the rodeo.

Photo: U.S.D.A.

Cattle Trails Led from Texas Ranges to Kansas Railroads

When Texas became part of the United States in 1845, efforts were intensified to find markets for the vast numbers of wild, unbranded cattle on the plains. Herds of them were driven to New Orleans and Mobile, with some going to Missouri, Iowa, Illinois, Ohio, Kentucky, and Tennessee. The northern drives were interrupted by the Civil War, when the cattle industry of the Southwest collapsed and herds again roamed at will. At the end of the war, Texas ranchers were "cattle poor," but a large demand for beef arose in the north to feed industrial workers and to supply the army engaged in Indian wars in the West. Cattle drives to eastern points were again undertaken and proved profitable despite losses to cattle thieves along the way.

Such sporadic cattle drives from Texas to uncertain destinations in the Middle West came to a sudden end in 1867, when an experienced and enterprising cattle dealer built stockyards at a hamlet in Kansas named Abilene, on the Kansas and Pacific Railroad and set up an efficient establishment for buying, selling and shipping cattle. Thus began the most dramatic phase of the western cattle industry in which thousands of cattle were driven by cowboys hundreds of miles over the broad prairie to cow-towns located on the railroads that were pushing ever westward across the Plains. In addition to supplying eastern markets and providing beef for frontier army posts and Reser-

CATTLE TRAILS NORTH FROM TEXAS, 1860-90

U. S. DEPARTMENT OF AGRICULTURE

vation Indians, Texas trail cattle furnished foundation stock for herds in Nebraska, the Dakotas, Colorado, Wyoming, Montana and beyond.

Map: U.S.D.A.

Dodge City, Kansas, as a Cowtown in 1878

The law-abiding citizens of Abilene, soon wearied of the turbulence connected with the cattle drives and asked that herds be taken elsewhere, as the people would "no longer submit to the evils of the trade."

Dodge City, Kansas, its successor, soon became noted for its violence.

Photo: Kansas State Historical Society

Wyatt Earp, Bat Masterson, and Other Frontier Officers and Men in 1883

The frontier was a haven for outlaws wanted for various crimes. Along with cowboys in town for a spree, buffalo hunters from the plains, trappers flush with a season's take, and prospectors wild with a "strike," they often made the frontier town a wild and dangerous place. To preserve order, each town elected a marshal, and each county a sheriff, but, as the hazards were great, usually only a person with an established reputation as a gunman could be induced to take the job.

A number of the men pictured above were outstanding at the desperate business of jerking a gun and shooting, "buffaloing" (knocking unconscious), or getting the drop on a man intent on vicious action. According to Merritt Beeson, who said he "cut his teeth on the poker chips of the old Long Branch Saloon in Dodge City," the noted peace officers and western characters pictured above are seated, left to right: Charlie Bassett, first sheriff of Ford County, Kansas; Wyatt Earp, who died of old age despite having served as marshal of such places as Wichita, Dodge City, and Tombstone when they were rated as the toughest towns on earth; Frank McLane, a Texas gambler; and Neal Brown, a race-horse partner of the famous sheriff Bill Tilghman. Standing left to right are: William H. Harris, owner, with Chalk Beeson, of the Long Branch Saloon in Dodge City; Luke Short, who was noted as the best dressed gunfighter in the West; and Bat Masterson, who at twenty-four was "the best sheriff of them all." This picture was taken in 1883 when the group, dressed in their "Sunday best," were serving as a Peace Commission for Dodge City.

Photo: National Archives

"Billy the Kid,"
Notorious Gunman of the Southwest

As the West became more settled, conflicts arose over possession of the range, originally between cattlemen, later between cattle and sheep ranchers, and finally between ranchers and farmers. The cattlemen, first to occupy the country, had battled Indians, wild animals, and the lack of markets, and once successful they had no intention of giving way to newcomers. To protect his "rights," the ranchman surrounded himself with hard-riding, quick-shooting cowboys who made his fight their fight. One of the most bloody of the range feuds was the so-called Lincoln County War in New Mexico, which raged over a two-year period and took the lives of several men. One faction engaged the services of a notorious young killer called "Billy the Kid," who had exceptional skill and speed with a gun. Later the Kid (William H. Bonney) was outlawed for wanton killings and shot by Pat Garrett, a former acquaintance turned sheriff.

Photo: New Mexico State Tourist Bureau

Frontier Trial

Law and order did not come easily to the frontier. In early days the individual was expected to protect his life and property as best he could. However, when cattle or horse thieves became bold, vigilance committees were organized, headed by a prominent citizen. When suspects were captured, a hurried "trial" was held, and, if found guilty violators were promptly hung. Such self-appointed vigilantes served a purpose during the period prior to establishment of regular courts, but their lack of judicious procedure occasionally resulted in injustice and the system was subject to abuse. Here two men are depicted during a frontier trial, the outcome of which they apparently feel will not be good for them.

Copyrighted print used with permission of Fred T. Darville

The Texas Rangers—Law and Order Was Their Business

Among noted frontier law-enforcement agencies, none exceeded that of the famous Texas Rangers, who, like the Royal Canadian Northwest Mounted Police, always got their man. To become a Ranger a man had to have great physical strength, unquestioned courage, keen eyesight, and superior ability with guns. To Captain W. J. (Bill) McDonald (opposite), a genial Scotsman so devoid of fear that his fellow Rangers claimed he would "charge hell with a bucket of water," is attributed the story that following an urgent request for a company of Rangers to quell a riot, McDonald got off the train at the scene alone. When outraged local authorities protested vehemently, McDonald replied calmly, "But isn't there only one riot?"

N. H. Rose Collection with special permission of Frontier Pix, copyright owner

Cowboys in a Montana Bunkhouse

at the End of a Day

Contrary to popular conceptions, the life of a cowboy was hard, monotonous, lonely, poorly paid, hazardous and unromantic. He spent long days alone "riding fence" or looking after cattle, sleeping on the ground exposed to elements. He ate coarse, poorly cooked food. Once a month or so he got to a town consisting of a few stores, a blacksmith shop, a dingy saloon, a weather-beaten hotel and little else. His salary of $30 or $40 a month went for a few clothes, tobacco, riding gear and, for some, a little whiskey and poker. Extremely loyal to his employer and friends, the cowboy went about his arduous tasks soberly and skillfully with none of the instincts of the gunmen so often depicted in "Western" movies.

Often, to quiet a restive herd, he would sing lonesome ballads in a quavering voice as he rode through the night. But the average cowboy was no musician. The picture below of a typical group of cowhands was taken in the log bunkhouse of the Diamond Ranch in Montana. The young man in the center, Frank Weinrich, had just returned from a trip to the city, hence the white shirt, tie and suit. The Diamond Ranch grazed 16,000 cattle over thousands of acres of land, of which all but 320 acres was public range.

Photo: Courtesy Fred F. Traeger

A Young Cowboy

Has His Picture Taken

In the 1880's this young cowboy put on his best finery, probably some of it borrowed for the occasion, and had his picture taken. Despite the theatrical appearance of his attire, each item from head to foot had its practical aspect. The large hat not only gave shelter from sun and rain but could be used to fan a slow campfire, as a water bucket, and the like. The scarf, or bandanna, around his neck had many uses; it could mop a brow or serve as a bandage, and when drawn over the nose and mouth it gave some protection from stifling dust on the trail. The heavy shirt absorbed perspiration during the day and gave warmth in the quick chill of nightfall. The blue denim overalls were close fitting to make it easy to slip on the tough leather chaps which protected the legs when one was riding through sagebrush, cactus, etc. The patch pockets on the chaps carried extra tobacco, cigarette papers, matches, cord, small tools, and other often needed equipment. The boots saved ankles from bruises and scratches, and their high heels prevented the foot from slipping through open stirrups with possible serious consequences. The vicious-looking spurs and the "curb bit" on the bridle helped control the wild cayuses ridden by cowboys. The six-shooters strapped around the waist and swinging free at the hip were at hand for quick use when the wearer was mounted or on foot. The lariat served a dozen purposes, the main one being to lasso a cow or calf for branding or dehorning. Like other features of the saddle, the horn served a definite purpose, to act as a "hitching post" when an animal was lassoed.

Photo: Historical Society of Montana

169

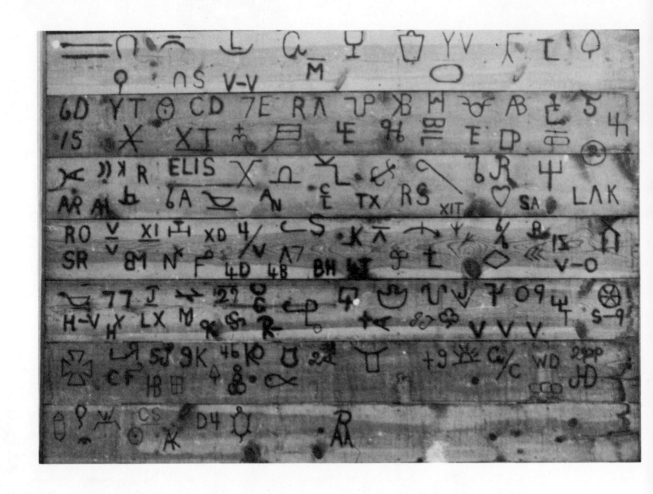

Cattle Brands are Strange Looking but Denote Ownership

To distinguish ownership of cattle during colonial days, the Spanish developed a system of brands, or marks, which were seared into the hide of cows in a prominent spot, usually on the flank or side of the animal. When the cattle industry moved north, branding was adopted by western ranchmen. The brands are designed by each individual and often take such curious shapes and designs that it is difficult to "read" them. Each state maintains a brand-registration book so that duplication of designs is avoided and the owner assured of a clear title to stock carrying his mark.

Photo: Wyoming State Historical Department

"Attack on the Stockade"

Usually in "western" movies about all the army ever does is to gallop up at the last desperate minute blowing bugles at the Indians as they disappear over a hill. Actually, most Indian fighting during the expansion westward was done by the army. Indian wars and conflicts were the training ground for American army officers from George Washington to John J. Pershing. Army life at the isolated posts on the fringe of civilization, or beyond, was lonely, hazardous, drab, and underpaid. During the Civil War, people of Spanish ancestry in the Southwest supported the Northern cause and many served in the Federal Army. This support helped tie the entire West to the Union. It was of particular significance in holding down marauding bands of Indians, who started roaming the West when forces at many of the regular army posts were recalled.

Photo: Collection of the Knoedler Galleries, New York

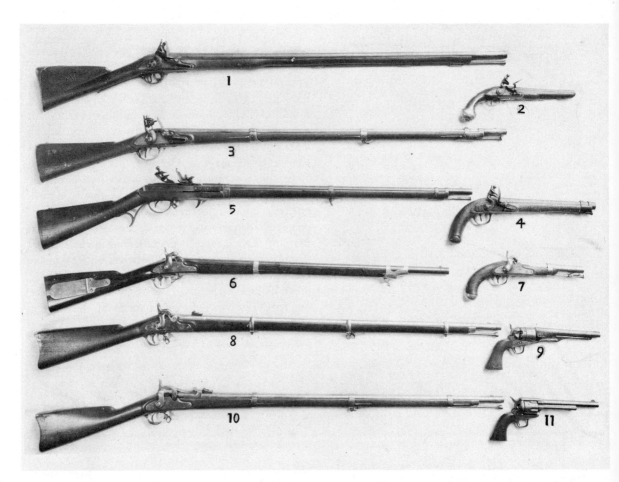

Some Typical Military Firearms

Revolutionary War

1. "British Brown Bess," a flintlock smoothbore musket used for over fifty years by British military forces including colonial militia in America. Most muskets issued to American forces in the Revolution were of this type.
2. Regulation British flintlock pistol used by both British and Americans during the Revolution.

War of 1812

3. American-made flintlock musket. Eli Whitney, the inventor of the cotton gin, made guns for the young republic under contract and is credited with being the founder of mass production involving the principle of interchangeable parts.
4. Muzzle-loading flintlock pistol model of 1811 made under government contract.

Seminole War, 1833–42

5. First U.S.-made breechloading rifle. Put out by the Harper's Ferry arsenal in 1819, it later was converted from a flintlock to a percussion type.

Mexican War, 1846–48

6. Percussion muzzle-loading rifle, U.S. model of 1841, later equipped with a sword bayonet.
7. Percussion muzzle-loading pistol model of 1842.

Civil War, 1861–65

8. Percussion-cap muzzle-loading rifle, 1861 model, used by both Northern and Southern forces.
9. Colt army revolver of 1861. Two calibers, .36 for the Navy and .44 for the Army.

Western Indian Wars

10. Civil War muzzle-loading rifle converted to breech-loader. Thousands of such leftover rifles were converted for use against the Indians in the Far West.
11. Colt army model of 1872, similar to the Peacemaker except for the longer barrel.

Photo: Smithsonian Institution

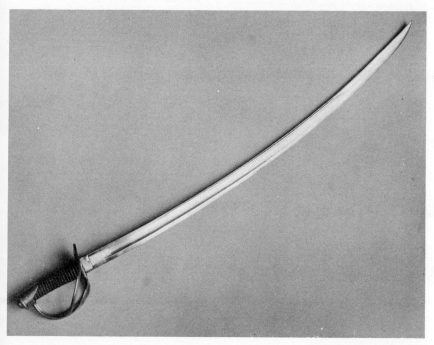

Cavalry Saber, Circa 1840

In the military history of America, principal types of swords were the long curving saber used in a cavalry charge and the short, thick-bladed cutlass used by sailors primarily in boarding operations. In colonial wars and during the Revolution, officers were not permitted sidearms, that they might not during battle be tempted to use them instead of concentrating on their proper function of directing maneuvers. General Washington ordered his officers to carry spears and swords for self-protection. Before repeating guns were available, swords were the soldier's main reliance after they had fired their single-shot weapons. The Indians' hit-and-run tactics made the sword of little use against them. The Civil War saw virtually the last use of the sword in this country as a military weapon.

Photo: Courtesy of Lt. Col. H. W. Williams, Jr., USAR

Naval Enlisted Man's Cutlass, 1860

Photo: Courtesy Harold L. Peterson

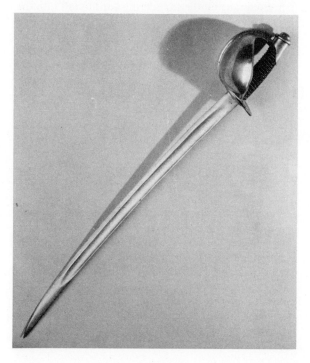

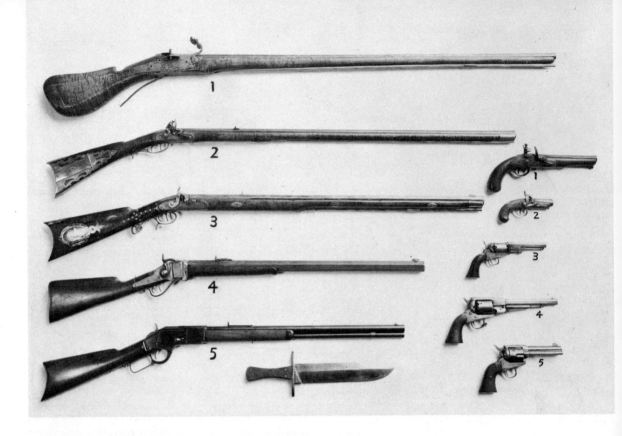

Typical Weapons used by Frontiersmen in the Winning of the West

1. *Colonial Musket.* A matchlock muzzle-loading smoothbore musket used about 1650 and typical of weapons in the colonial period. A piece of string attached to the lever was lighted with flint and steel, the gun was then aimed, and the trigger depressed causing the smoldering cord to fall into the pan containing powder. The resulting flash ignited powder in the barrel.

2. *Kentucky Long Rifle.* The powerful, straight-shooting flintlock weapon developed in Pennsylvania from a similar but heavier firearm brought from Germany. When the trigger was pressed, the piece of flint held in the jaws of the lock struck the steel cover of the flash pan, creating a shower of sparks which ignited the powder in the pan and in turn the powder in the barrel. The spiral rifling inside the barrel gave a spin to the bullet, which kept it on a straighter course than did the old smoothbore musket.

3. *Plains Percussion Rifle.* When the plains country was reached, frontiersmen generally hunted and traveled on horseback. This rifle was developed to meet their needs. The Plains Rifle had the percussion firing system, in which a copper cap containing an explosive compound was inserted over a nipple covering a hole into the barrel. When the trigger was depressed the hammer struck the copper cap, causing an explosion which touched off the powder in the barrel.

4. *Sharps Buffalo Rifle,* "The Old Reliable." Usually .44-caliber, this heavy breech-loading rifle was used for hunting buffalo.

5. *Winchester '73.* A short, rugged, powerful, easy to handle repeating rifle that became one of the most famous of all Western weapons. It fitted snugly into a scabbard attached to a saddle and was a favorite of Buffalo Bill Cody and other plainsmen.

REVOLVERS

1. Typical flintlock pistol used in late colonial and Revolutionary periods.

2. Derringer. A small, compact, .45-caliber pistol, much favored by gamblers. It was a deadly weapon at close range and could be carried in a vest pocket.

3. Colt Pocket or Belt Pistol. Popular in the gold fields of 1849, this model was also a favorite with Wells-Fargo drivers and guards.

4. Remington Revolver. A Civil War percussion pistol that was popular with postwar Western settlers.

5. Colt Frontier Revolver. The "shooting iron" most often used by Western cowboys, gunmen, sheriffs, and marshals.

Bowie Knife. Designed by James Bowie, famous western hunter and fighter, this is a vicious but effective weapon at close range. It served many purposes for the hunter, trapper, and ranchman.

Photo: Smithsonian Institution

Range Sheep Industry in New Mexico

As Texas was the founder of the range cattle industry in the United States, so New Mexico was the mother of our range sheep business, which is older than cattle ranching. It has been carried on for over two hundred years by the inhabitants of the Southwest. Coronado, in his fruitless search for gold in inhospitable deserts and plains, left behind a few sheep which, with others obtained from later expeditions and colonization efforts, was the start of sheep raising in the West. Gradually flocks increased and their numbers spread throughout the Southwest, California, and southern Colorado during the long Spanish period before that area became a part of the United States. After the Civil War, when railroads provided essential transportation to markets, sheep raising spread slowly to the mountain states and the plains area in the face of bitter opposition from cattlemen, who argued that sheep would ruin the range by close grazing. Lonely sheepherders with their wagons containing a bunk, cookstove, and other necessaries, acompanied by trained dogs, follow flocks of about twelve hundred sheep as they graze across the vast range country of the West. Basque sheepherders from Spain still watch their herds on the grasslands of Idaho.

Photo: USDA

New Discoveries of Gold and Silver in the West
Kept Prospectors Rushing from Place to Place

The discovery of gold in California in 1848 was followed ten years later by a small strike in Colorado which touched off a "Pike's Peak or Bust" gold rush involving a hundred thousand wild-eyed prospectors, most of whom went back home again within a few months, sadder and perhaps wiser. Subsequent important discoveries were made in Colorado (especially of silver at Leadville in 1879) and in Nevada, where the fabulous Comstock Lode was unearthed in 1859; in Idaho, 1860; Arizona, 1858; Montana, 1862–64; Wyoming, 1867; South Dakota, 1874; and Idaho again in 1883. As each new find was announced, a mad rush would be on, as here depicted by a miner making a frantic departure for the Black Hills of South Dakota.

Print: Library of Congress

Denver, Colorado, Was Once a Mining Camp

Gold rushes here and there throughout the West always included some miners who, after a time, decided to stay in the area and farm the rich, well-watered valleys or go into livestock ranching. Thus agriculture followed in the wake of the miners and in time became more important than all the minerals taken from the ground. Denver, Colorado, got its start as a mining camp but within a half dozen years was depicted (above) as a city of substantial buildings and broad streets. In less than a century, Denver has grown from a cluster of tents to a beautiful city of some five hundred thousand inhabitants.

Photo: Library of Congress

Streets of Helena, Montana in 1870

Throughout the West, mining camps, trading posts, and cowtowns were growing up. Many of them, almost overnight, became thriving business centers and permanent cities. Here in Helena, Montana, a few years after a weary and discouraged miner discovered gold in Last Chance Gulch in 1864, can be seen the transition from ramshackle structures at the far end of the street to two-story wooden buildings in the center of town with substantial buildings of brick and stone in the foreground. The freighting outfit drawn by ten horses and mules is typical of those used for long hauls before being replaced by the railroad. Many Western cities enjoy wide streets today because they were originally laid out so that six-, eight-, and ten-horse teams could turn around in them without backing.

Photo: National Archives

Building the First Railroad Across the Vast West

As migration crossed the Alleghenies and spread across the reaches of the West, transportation became paramount. The steamboat was important on many navigable rivers west to the Great Plains, but inter-river transportation required serviceable wagon roads, which cost so much that national, state, and local legislative bodies were reluctant to provide them. Further, freighting by team over long distances was often not economically feasible, hence, the enthusiasm for railroads. Beyond the Missouri River, where navigable waters were practically nonexistent, distances great, mountains high, population scarce, and markets a long way off, railroad transportation was essential before extensive settlement was possible.

At the outbreak of the Civil War in 1861, not a single mile of railroad lay west of the Missouri River, although east of the "Big Muddy" were more than thirty thousand miles of track. In 1863, construction got under way with the Union Pacific railroad building west from Omaha, Nebraska, and the Central Pacific heading east from San Francisco. Six years later, after having overcome terrific engineering problems, the job was done and the first transcontinental railroad was in operation. The days of the exhausting overland trip by horse or plodding oxen or long sea trip " 'Round the Horn" were over, and passengers could make the three-thousand-mile trip from coast to coast in comfort in a week's time.

Photo: Southern Pacific Company

Driving the Golden Spike in 1869

On May 10, 1869, at Promontory, Utah, a train from the East and one from the West, each loaded with distinguished sightseers, came to a stop a few feet apart and, while a crowd including construction workers, Indians, and cowboys looked on, Leland Stanford, Governor of California, drove the last spike, one specially made of gold. The next twenty-five years saw additional lines built to the coast with many branches and connecting links throughout the West. In 1881 the Atchison, Topeka, and Santa Fe crossed New Mexico and Arizona into southern California; two years later the Southern Pacific completed its line from New Orleans to San Francisco; the same year (1883) the Northern Pacific linked Chicago and Seattle with steel rails, and in 1893 the Great Northern similarly joined the Great Lakes and Puget Sound. When the railroads began to move out across the plains, through the Rockies, and on to the Pacific Coast, they were, for the first time, ahead of the population movement. Instead of building toward settled areas and providing services for established communities, they laid out the path of future development and, to help create a sustained and profitable traffic, entered into a period of railroad colonization.

Railroad building was expensive, and to encourage construction across the country and into thinly populated areas the federal government extended grants of land to railroad companies, which caused bitter feeling over a period of years. Settlers claimed that the railroads got the land free, sold it to farmers at a high profit, then charged exorbitant freight rates for hauling the farmers' produce to market. The railroads countered that the land was not an outright gift but that they agreed to certain concessions including the hauling of United States troops, government property, and mail at reduced rates. Under these terms the railroad companies obtained some one hundred and thirty-one million acres of land valued at the time at $123,000,000, or 94 cents per acre. During the ensuing near century, until the provisions were repealed by Congress in 1946, the land-grant railroads contributed around $1,250,000,000 in payment for the land or about ten times their original valuation. Looking back, it appears clear that without government assistance the railroads would not have been built. Without them, the West as we know it could not have been developed.

Photo: Union Pacific Railroad

Buffalo Bill

William H. Cody, at sixteen a Pony Express rider,
spent years on the plains, becoming an Indian scout
and adding to his fame by killing Yellow Hand, an
Indian Chief, in a hand-to-hand fight. Ned Buntline,
a writer of Western "true" adventures, made Cody's
name a household word and gave him the nickname
"Buffalo Bill" because of his prowess as a buffalo
hunter when providing meat for railroad workers. A
tall, athletic, handsome man with a flair for the dramatic and a fondness for fancy clothes, Cody went
into show business and thrilled audiences at home
and abroad with his Wild West show, some of the
feature attractions being "bronco-busting," an Indian
attack on a stagecoach, and the trick shooting done by
Buffalo Bill and a girl named Annie Oakley.

Photo: National Archives

"Custer's Last Stand" 1876

During the 250 years following the first permanent settlements along the Atlantic Coast, Indians had been pushed steadily West. On the Great Plains in the 1870's they were making their last desperate efforts to maintain the wild nomadic life they loved so well. The buffalo and other wild game upon which the Indian depended had virtually disappeared, leaving him the hard choice of accepting the white man's ways or confining himself to a reservation where a semblance of the old order could be maintained. Outnumbered and overpowered by superior weapons, the Indians stayed on the reservations until their resentment, bitterness and frustration boiled over and they again took to the warpath.

One of the last and certainly most dramatic conflicts occurred in 1876 when General George A. Custer and his force of 265 men were wiped out by 2,500 rampaging Indians in the valley of the Little Big Horn River in Montana. It is sometimes overlooked, however, that Custer's Last Stand was also the Indian's Last Stand. The massacre of General Custer and his men marked the end of the frontier era and signaled the opening of a new one in which the farmer and the factory worker were to have their day.

Photo: Library of Congress

General George A. Custer

Photo: National Archives

Chief Sitting Bull

Chief Sitting Bull was the strong and resourceful leader of the Sioux in the fight against Custer. The warriors had left their reservation when gold was discovered on it and thousands of white men had rushed in, totally disregarding the rights of the Indians.

Photo: National Archives

Back to the Reservations

Following these last sanguinary conflicts, the Indians retired to reservations, which were simply huge tracts of land set aside for their exclusive use. The idea of establishing reservations where Indians could live apart unmolested by white men was an old one in American Indian policy. It was predicated on the assumption that reservations would eliminate, or at least greatly reduce, friction and strife between the two groups and permit older Indians to continue life as before while the younger ones developed a different viewpoint which would enable them and later generations to make the transition to a new culture and gradually be absorbed into the general community. The Office of Indian Affairs in the Department of the Interior was created to look after the Indians' wel-fare, protect them from unscrupulous white men, train them in agriculture, forestry, and livestock raising, and provide them with educational facilities and medical attention.

Photo: USDI Indian Bureau

Herding Sheep on an Indian Reservation

Pueblo Indians of the Southwest had tended flocks of sheep for generations and Indians on reservations took up this practice, which gave them a way of life in many respects not greatly different from what they had experienced earlier.

Photo: USIS by Milton Snow

Reservation Indians Branding Cattle

Raising range cattle was another type of livelihood that appealed to Indians. Here, Hopi and Navaho Indians are branding a steer with both individual and tribal brands.

There are over four hundred thousand Indians in the United States and, with better health conditions, their number is increasing. It simply is not true that they are the "vanishing Indians." They have the right to vote and, of course, are not required to live on reservations, although many do in order to obtain various types of governmental aid and because they enjoy the easy life. Indians are encouraged to live elsewhere and it appears that reservations will soon be extinct.

Photo: USIS by Milton Snow

Indians Make Outstanding American Soldiers

Indians are still good fighters but now as officers and soldiers of the United States Armed Forces. Their record as fearless and devoted soldiers is outstanding, and the proportion of volunteers was high before the draft was inaugurated in World War II. One of the men who helped raise the flag on Iwo Jima was an Indian of the Pima tribe. When a couple of these stalwart young men carry on a conversation over a field telephone in the Apache or other Indian language, there is no fear of the message's being intercepted and translated by the enemy.

Photo: USIS

The Machine Age and the Great Plains

During the era of the open range, a rancher had no choice but to allow his cattle to roam more or less at will over a large area searching for grazing but within walking distance of water in a stream or occasional pond. Extensive fencing with wood, stone, or live hedges was not practical: to build fences of wood was economically impossible, there was not enough stone available, and, generally, moisture was insufficient to raise hedges. Finally, in the 1870's, barbed wire was invented. Cattle could now be restrained and pastures established, thus permitting rotation of grazing areas. Concurrently, windmills were developed, along with efficient well-digging equipment, thus enabling the ranchers to provide water for his stock almost any-

where and emancipating him from the relatively few "natural" water sources, such as streams and rivers. With railroad transportation to a choice of markets, the cattleman of the plains was finally in a position to exert considerable control over his operations and to manipulate them with intelligent planning.

Here in one picture are most of the elements which contributed to the development of the cattle industry on the Great Plains—grass, mounted herdsmen, windmills for pumping water, and the barbed-wire fence.

Photo: USDA
Photo: Smithsonian Institution

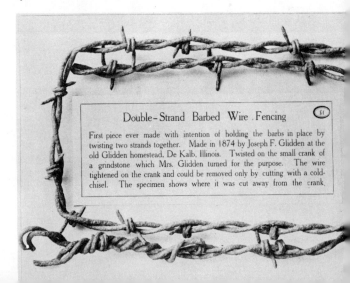

Double-Strand Barbed Wire Fencing

First piece ever made with intention of holding the barbs in place by twisting two strands together. Made in 1874 by Joseph F. Glidden at the old Glidden homestead, De Kalb, Illinois. Twisted on the small crank of a grindstone which Mrs. Glidden turned for the purpose. The wire tightened on the crank and could be removed only by cutting with a cold-chisel. The specimen shows where it was cut away from the crank.

"The Last of the Five Thousand"

One of the great hazards of the plains cattleman are the terrible snowstorms or blizzards that sometimes rage for days over wide areas. In the era of the open range, a blizzard could easily mean disaster, for herds were wiped out by days of heavy snow and subzero temperatures. At such times the herd would drift with the biting wind at its back and many cattle, blinded by snow, would go to destruction over cliffs; others, exhausted by exertion and lack of food, would sink into a snow drift and die.

In the bitter winter of 1886, Charles M. Russell, later renowned as one of the West's most famous artists, was a cowboy on a Montana ranch. During a severe blizzard the ranch foreman received an inquiry from the owner in town about his herd. Russell, using a piece of cardboard, drew the picture above of an exhausted cow stumbling through the snow with wolves closing in for the kill. The foreman sent the picture to his boss as an adequate reply. The picture became famous throughout the West.

Photo: Montana Stockgrowers' Association

The Great Free Press on the Frontier

The exciting story of the taming of the West was told in daily dispatches from the ever-present news reporter. Often, in boom towns and mining camps, the newspaper office was nothing more than a hurriedly constructed shack, or a tent like this one. The *Daily Reporter,* it will be noted, had a woman on its staff. The life of a newspaper editor was rough and sometimes dangerous. Most of them printed the truth as they saw it and that could mean real trouble in the turbulent days of the frontier. Many famous writers got their start in the West, including Mark Twain, Eugene Field, Bret Harte, and Jack London.

Photo: Montana State Historical Museum

The First Homestead Filed under Act of 1862

When the Revolutionary War was over in 1783, the new republic possessed millions of acres of land from which it derived needed revenue by disposing of large blocks to individuals and private concerns who in turn sold smaller tracts to eager young farmers. To the landless poor, it seemed that government land belonged to everybody and that anyone who would make productive use of the land ought to be given enough for his needs. Accordingly, many of them simply moved onto land of their choice and claimed it as their own on the basis of "squatter's rights." Finally in 1862 the Homestead Act was passed by Congress, essentially legalizing the principle of squatter's rights. It gave 160 acres of the public domain to any adult citizen (or one who had filed his intention of becoming a citizen of this country), provided he paid a small fee, lived on the land for five years, and carried out certain cultivation practices. Homesteads were granted to over a million settlers, many of whom were immigrants from abroad, especially Germans, Russians, Czechs, Poles, and Scandinavians.

Shown above is the pioneer home of Daniel Freeman, near Beatrice, Nebraska, on the first homestead filed under the Act of 1862. On the relatively unproductive remaining land of the West, farmers could not make a satisfactory living on 160 acres and grants were increased to 320 acres, and finally to 640 acres.

Actually the Homestead Act was only a partial success; it was neither carefully drawn nor effectively administered and was passed so late in the history of western settlement that very little desirable land remained in the public domain. The largest acreage was taken up during World War I when thirty-nine million acres were acquired. The Homestead Act eliminated further use of public land as bounty for war veterans, a practice in vogue since colonial wars; under various bounty acts passed from 1776 to 1855, more than seventy-three million acres were awarded to war veterans. Curiously, one of the first uses of public land in the United States was as an inducement to entice Germans serving in the British Army during the Revolution to desert.

Photo: Beatrice, Nebraska, Chamber of Commerce

In 1880 the "Golden West" Needed People

At the close of the Civil War, the West had great natural resources ripe for development. For this purpose, people—lots of people—were needed. Land was available to settlers under the Homestead Act of 1862 and states, railroads, and private land companies had millions of acres for sale at low prices on easy terms. All of these agencies made strenuous efforts to encourage emigration to the West. Lecturers toured the East and Europe extolling the wonders to be seen and the riches to be had for the taking. Posters and pamphlets depicted the land of opportunity in glowing terms with no semblance of false modesty. This advertisement, used in 1880, put the proposition flatly: "Where to go to become rich."

Print: Kansas State Historical Society

Every Western State Advertised Its Glorious Future

States offered free homes in bountiful and progressive communities which could boast a state university, college of agriculture, school of mines, two colleges for teachers, school for deaf mutes, soldiers' home, hospital for the insane, state penitentiary, and a reform school.

Photo: Library of Congress

Emigrants Headed for the West

The entrancing story of the new land of opportunity was heard, listened to, and acted upon by thousands of immigrants, most of them from Europe, who poured into the Golden West. Enthused by what they saw, the immigrants themselves became propagandists, and countless letters to friends and relatives in the "home country" boosted immigration. Several nationalities are included in this picture taken on the Central Pacific Railroad (now Southern Pacific) at Mill City, Nevada, in the early 1880's. The immigrants traveled at a special low fare in passenger cars attached to freight trains.

A Sod House on the Plains

Man has always found material for building a home, whether with palm branches of the South Pacific or ice blocks of the frozen North. On the Great Plains settlers used thick, tough sod—the very earth itself. Strips a foot wide, three feet long, and four or five inches thick were piled up to form the walls on which was placed a wooden roof or, since boards were scarce, more frequently a framework of poles covered with turf. Such houses were warm in winter, cool in summer, practically cyclone-proof, and never burned down. Interiors were usually left unfinished; however, they were sometimes sealed with a plaster of clay and ashes.

Structures built of sod were veritable fortresses. In one instance, the so-called Battle of Adobe Walls, the success of twenty-eight frontier sharpshooters in standing off several hundred Indians was attributed in part to the fact that the beleaguered buildings had thick walls of sod.

Photo: Oklahoma State Historical Society

Opening of the Cherokee Strip

Much of the area now constituting the state of Oklahoma had been set aside by Congress as a permanent home for several tribes of Indians, but continual pressure for opening the area to settlers under the Homestead Act resulted in still another deal with the Indians followed by probably the greatest land rush of all time. It was announced that at noon on April 22, 1889, anyone who wished to do so could enter portions of the previously forbidden area and stake a claim. On the appointed day thousands of people lined the border on horseback, in wagons, buggies, bicycles, and various other means of transportation, ready at the signal to rush in and grab a piece of land. All along the line troops were stationed to keep the "Sooners" from jumping the gun. When the signal sounded, the wild race was on and before nightfall millions of acres of land were claimed; Oklahoma City and Guthrie had populations of ten to fifteen thousand where before had been only wide open spaces. This exciting procedure was re-enacted in opening the Cherokee Strip (on September 16, 1893), and elsewhere until all of the present state was settled.

Print: Library of Congress

Pioneer Woman

Since the days of Jamestown and Plymouth, the life of the American woman has been unlike that of her sisters elsewhere. In Europe almost everyone lived in a town where help and companionship were always close at hand and life was safe and secure. The pioneer woman enjoyed no such existence and her life was one of isolation, often in the midst of a frightening forest or on the lonesome prairie where wild animals roamed and savage Indians lurked. Her home was a crude shelter containing a few homemade pieces of furniture and lighted by candles of her own making. Neighbors were few and widely spaced, perhaps miles away, and her main contact with the outside world was from an occasional traveler or an itinerant preacher. Her children were born without aid of doctor or even a midwife, and when sickness came she simply did the best she could with the aid of her husband and some "old-fashioned remedies." Cooking over an open fire with heavy, crude utensils, washing clothes on a rock in a creek, making soap from animal fat, caring for her large brood of children and working in the fields made up the day-by-day round of these dauntless women.

Despite all this, the pioneer woman was no galley slave but, with courage high and hope aflame, was determined to improve her lot and to make her mark on the page of history.

Photo: Copyright and courtesy of the sculptor, Bryant Baker

The Little Brown Church in the Vale

Come Sunday morning, people somewhere will be singing the praises of the "Little Brown Church in the Vale." They may not know it, but they are singing about this country church in a peaceful little valley along the Cedar River in Iowa which has sixty thousand visitors and more than a thousand weddings each year. About two-thirds of the American people belong to some church, most of which are quite simple, unpretentious structures. From various lands, immigrants brought their faiths with them to the East Coast and then across the wide stretches of the U.S.A.

Photo: Iowa Development Commission

LEAVENING THE LOAF

The development of manufacturing machinery and application of water power about 1750 gave England an advantage which she attempted to retain by restricting exportation of machines and blueprints. However, men with exceptional memories for mechanical details debarked for America to accept proffered awards for reconstruction of machines they had helped to build and operate in England. After the War for Independence, the industrial revolution spread out across the world and found fertile ground in young and energetic America, where intellectual curiosity, mechanical skill, and individual resourcefulness had been given opportunity for nearly two hundred years.

Inventors received a tremendous incentive when President Washington signed a bill which, for the first time in history, established the right of an inventor to profit by his genius and to enjoy certain inalienable privileges. In 1844, the Commissioner of Patents thought that "the advancement of the arts seems to presage the arrival of that period when human improvement must end." However, since then more than two million patents have been granted. By the eve of the Civil War, scientifically minded men using the accumulated knowledge of the ages and their own genius had created works that were to change the lives of generations yet unborn. Depicted below is a group of American inventors whose lives fit into a common pattern of poor boy, a hard-earned education, an original idea that persisted until resolved, and success in lifting mankind an inch or so off its hands and knees.

Seated left to right are: Charles Goodyear—rubber; Jordan L. Mott—works in iron, fuel; Dr. Eliphalet Mott —management heat; Frederick E. Sickles—steam cutoff; Samuel Finley Breese Morse—electric telegraph; Henry Burden—horseshoe machine; Richard March Hoe—rotary press; Isaiah Jennings—friction matches; Thomas Blanchard—extension lathe; Elias Howe—sewing machine.

Standing left to right: Cyrus Hall McCormick—reapers; Joseph Saxton—Mint & Coast Survey; Dr. Wm. Thomas Green Morton—etherization; James Bogardus— iron architecture; Samuel Colt—revolvers; Peter Cooper —gelatin; Joseph Henry—electro-magnetic motor; John Ericson—caloric engine; Erastus Brigham Bigelow— power loom.

Print: National Archives

First Commissioner of Agriculture and Staff, 1862

During the 269 years between the Jamestown Settlement of 1607 and Custer's Last Stand in 1876, the major agricultural problem was opening up the land to homemakers, clearing forests, driving off Indians, and getting people onto the land where they could create homes and farms. But now the time had come to increase agricultural output per acre, per animal, and per man rather than simply bringing more and more land under cultivation. The new objective would require research, experimentation, demonstration, and diffusion of knowledge of better farming practices. As the first step toward accomplishing these goals, the Congress established the United States Department of Agriculture in 1862 with Isaac Newton (seated center) as the first Commissioner of Agriculture. The ten men pictured here represented one third of the entire department staff in 1867. At Mr. Newton's left is J. R. Dodge, the first American "foreign trainee." In 1873, he was sent to Europe to study the statistical methods being used, with special attention to those that might be found useful in the United States.

Photo: USDA

"Old Main" at Iowa State College

The land-grant college is a vibrant symbol of democracy in education. Devoted to fulfillment of human needs and the especial wants of the common man, it has achieved success through close federal-state cooperation in a fearless search by scientific methods for answers to a wide range of problems. Passage of the Morrill Act in 1862 extending government aid to higher education through establishment of land-grant colleges was a departure from traditional concepts and was surrounded by many doubts, including skepticism about the value of teaching science and the application of scientific methods to agriculture and the mechanic arts. Bitter struggles over a site for the college within a state was only one of many problems afflicting early institutions. Qualified teachers were rare and none had been trained to teach agriculture. Few versed in science had the farm background that enabled them to relate theory and practice. Practical farmers, although personally skilled, lacked the necessary scientific knowledge. Before success came, teaching methods, textbooks, and training materials had to be developed, scientists convinced that their discoveries should be disseminated for the general good, and farmers and other skeptics convinced that science could be of practical use. Actually it was not until a quarter of a century later when experiment stations demonstrated the unmistakable benefits to be gained from a scientific approach that the land-grant colleges became really effective. Engineering schools were not plagued by such difficulties and during early years made much more rapid progress and were more effective than their companion, the agricultural school. Many colleges, hoping to dignify manual labor and to balance scientific learning with practical knowledge, required students to perform farm work as a part of the curriculum, for which they were usually recompensed at about eight cents an hour. The provision that military tactics be taught no doubt stemmed from the fact that the Land-Grant College Act was passed in the midst of a war. As finally evolved, only about 12 per cent of the students at land-grant colleges are enrolled in agriculture. The land-grant college catered to what Jefferson called "the aristocracy of talents and virtue" without regard to social or economic background.

The Iowa legislature apparently was the first to accept the provisions of the Morrill Land-Grant College Act on September 11, 1862. The college received students for preparatory training October 21, 1868, and the formal opening, with the dedication of the first building and the inauguration of the first president, was on March 17, 1869. Shown above is a picture of "Old Main," completed in 1870 as the first building on the campus of Iowa State College. Michigan State College, founded in 1855, was the first agricultural college; land-grant institutions patterned much of their early work on its experiences.

Photo: Iowa State College Information Service

Founders of the "Patrons of Husbandry"

In 1867, the first large privately supported farm organization was established, marking the beginning of farm groups devoted to the welfare of the agricultural community. Today they count their members in the millions. The gentlemen pictured above founded the "Patrons of Husbandry," better known as the Grange. The Farmers' Union was founded in 1902, followed by the American Farm Bureau Federation in 1920.

Photo: Courtesy of the Grange

First College Football Game; Rutgers 6, Princeton 4

From early colonial days, Americans have been interested in hunting, fishing, horseback riding, swimming, and other essentially individual sports. Horse racing, wrestling, boxing, shooting matches, badger baiting, cock fighting, dog racing, and similar sporting events have enjoyed attention throughout our history. Group sports intended primarily to entertain the spectator developed late in the nineteenth century after the mass of people had acquired leisure and surplus funds and when transportation facilities made competition between distant rivals possible and attendance at isolated playing fields easy.

On November 6, 1869, at New Brunswick, New Jersey, Rutgers University played Princeton University in the first college football game and inaugurated a type of contest that despite slow progress for several decades finally has grown to be a giant of the sports world. The below composite picture shows the members of the Rutgers 1869 team. In the center is William James Leggett, captain. Presumably whisker pulling was forbidden.

Photo: Rutgers Sports

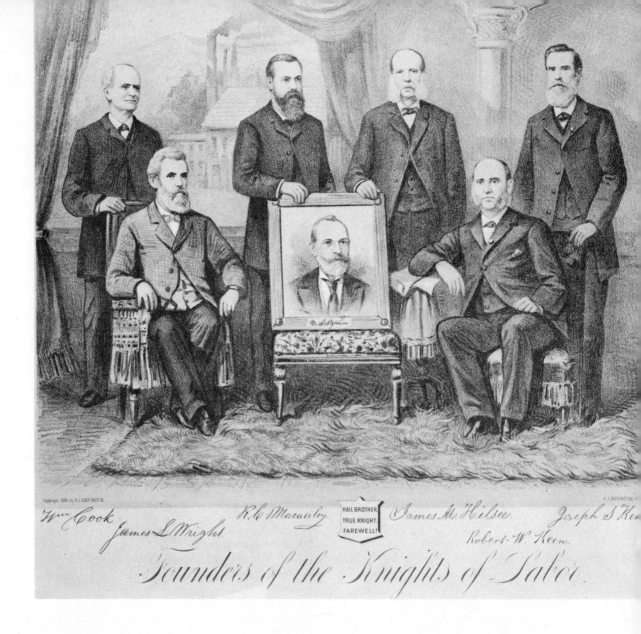

Copyright 1886 by H.J.SKEFFINGTON

H.J.SKEFFINGTON P.

Wm Cook

R.C Macauley

HAIL BROTHER. TRUE KNIGHT. FAREWELL!

James M Hilsee

Joseph S Ken

James L Wright

Robert W Keen.

Founders of the Knights of Labor

Toward a Higher Living Standard

The rapid rise of the factory system after 1820 resulted in bad working conditions, the consequences of which were not fully recognized for some time by either management or labor. Working long hours on the farm and in the family shop had been customary, and the evil effects of similar hours in poorly lighted and grimy factories were not readily apparent. The theory of "rugged individualism" then generally accepted meant equally the freedom of the employer to run his business to suit himself and the freedom of the employee to accept conditions or quit. As factories became larger and more prosperous, the owner became increasingly strong in public affairs and further removed from personal relationship with his employees. In this situation working conditions deteriorated and it became difficult to correct them. Efforts to improve wages and working conditions culminated in the formation of a workers' organization, the Knights of Labor, in 1869. Previous attempts at unionism had been largely confined to setting up local craft groups, but the Knights of Labor endeavored to incorporate all workers, both skilled and unskilled, in one national organization. The movement fell of its own weight, being too large and cumbersome and embracing too many irresponsible units to be truly effective. It did, however, accomplish some worthwhile results and was a forward step in the long struggle for a higher standard of living for working people.

Photo: Library of Congress

Building Occupied by the Bureau of Labor, 1884

In the history of every new development, movement, or worth-while invention in this country there has been a time lag between its initial inception and final success, peak performance, or general acceptance. Years passed before the McCormick reaper came into common use; a whole generation passed, after the first appropriation to aid agriculture, before a Commissioner was appointed, and another quarter of a century rolled by before the position was raised to cabinet status. And so it was with the Department of Labor. The first effort, a failure, was made in 1865 and only after almost twenty years and many defeats was a bill put through Congress to establish a Bureau of Labor. It was more than twenty-five years later that a separate department of cabinet rank was established. The act creating the Labor Department stated its purpose "shall be to foster, promote, and develop the welfare of wage earners of the United States, to improve their working conditions, and to advance their opportunities for profitable employment." Starting as a bureau, headed by Commissioner Carroll D. Wright, with a few employees, in this building at Fifteenth Street and New York Avenue, N.W., Washington, in 1884, the labor agency gradually expanded until the demands placed on it by World War I caused rapid growth and expansion into many new fields. After World War II and the Korean conflict, the Department of Labor had about five thousand employees engaged in a wide range of activities including employment security, labor standards, wage and hour regulations, and employee compensation acts, all designed primarily in the interest of the nation's more than sixty million workers.

Photo: U.S. Department of Labor

Country School, 1888

On the last day of the term in 1888 at the Brush Creek School near Ottumwa, Iowa, children were dressed in their best Sunday clothes because a photographer was coming out from the city to take their picture. Both older and younger brothers and sisters of the students came to school that day and some neighborhood men who were cutting wood nearby also got into the picture. The stout hickory stick clasped firmly in the teacher's hands was her symbol of authority and was quite meaningful in a day when the maxim, "Spare the rod and spoil the child," was almost universally accepted. There was nothing fancy about these one-room, poorly equipped country schools. But it was public schools such as this which played such a large part in reducing illiteracy and which provided the basic knowledge of reading, writing, and arithmetic upon which was built the more advanced and complex educational system of today.

Photo: Courtesy Class of 1888

Luther Burbank

Progress in the fruit, flower, and vegetable industries in California and throughout the country was
pushed forward by the work of Luther Burbank, a
self-taught plant breeder. During the fifty-three years
from 1873 to 1926, Burbank introduced more new
plants than any other person in American history.
His mass breeding methods and poor record-keeping
make it impossible to determine accurately the exact
number of plants he contributed, but he is credited
with introducing over two hundred varieties of fruits
alone.

Photo: Library of Congress

Thomas A. Edison

The age of science had its greatest American exponent in Thomas A. Edison (1847–1931), who was born in Ohio of poor parents and as a boy was considered so stupid in school that he was taught at home by his mother. At twelve he sold newspapers on a train and during slack periods carried on chemical experiments in the baggage car until a fire resulted and he was discharged after having his ears slapped so hard that eventually he became deaf. Edison learned telegraphy and made numerous improvements in equipment which he patented and sold. With this financial start while only twenty-two, he was able to devote more than fifty years to invention and scientific research. Among his many achievements and improvements were the first phonograph, storage battery, synthetic rubber, motion pictures, and, probably greatest invention of all, the incandescent lamp.

Photo: National Archives

From Candle to Electric Light

Throughout history, efforts had been made to provide better light with the results indicated below by the (1) brass candlestick—around 1500, (2) wrought-iron grease lamp—about 1700, (3) brass whale-oil lamp—1800–40, (4) pewter camphine lamp—1830–65, (5) brass lard lamp—patented 1842, (6) pressed-glass kerosene lamp—patented 1854 (this one about 1870), and (7) gas burner—about 1860. When Edison issued the electric lamp in 1880, all of these lighting devices became obsolete. Installation of electric lights in private homes was retarded by the fear of many people that they might be electrocuted. Not until 1891 were they placed in the White House.

Photo: Smithsonian Institution

The Pure Food and Drugs Act

As the nation matured, more and more demands were placed upon the government for additional services. In 1800 there were only 125 employees of the federal government, but this number had increased to 7,000 in 1860. By 1884 the need for work in chemistry on behalf of agriculture resulted in the creation of the Bureau of Chemistry, headed by Dr. Harvey W. Wiley, the tall, bearded gentleman third from the right, surrounded by his staff. When the Pure Food and Drugs Act was passed in 1906, enforcement of the law was made the responsibility of the Bureau of Chemistry. In 1912 Dr. Wiley resigned from the government but continued to write and work in behalf of proper preparation, packaging, and labeling of food and drugs.

Photo: USDA

Samuel Gompers

In 1881, a group of trade unionists organized the American Federation of Labor to represent them in matters involving more than one trade union or group of workers. Samuel Gompers, born in 1850 in London of parents born in Holland, was elected president of the American Federation of Labor and, except for one year, served in that capacity until his death in 1924. During his lifetime, Gompers saw the labor movement grow from intermittent, uncoordinated clusters of discontent to a highly organized and powerful social, economic and political force. Samuel Gompers devoted his dynamic energy and brilliant mind to furtherance of his creed that "trade unions are the organizations of the working class, for the working class, by the working class; grappling with economic and social problems as they arise, dealing with them in a practical manner to the end that a solution commensurate with the interests of all may be obtained."

Photo: American Federation of Labor

Southington, Connecticut, Free Public Library

It has been the good fortune of this country to have men of great wealth who were public spirited and who considered it their duty to devote a sizable portion of their wealth to the common good. The list of such benefactors is a long one, including Rockefellers, Guggenheims, Fords, Kelloggs, and Mellons. These and others represent an honorable and unique chapter in the annals of rich men of the world.

Andrew Carnegie (1835–1919), a Scotch emigrant, who made hundreds of millions of dollars in steel and then used it for public libraries and other good works, expressed this philosophy in these words: "This, then, is held to be the duty of the man of wealth: To set an example of modest, unostentatious living, shunning display or extravagance; to provide moderately for the legitimate wants of those dependent upon him; and, after doing so, to consider all surplus revenues which come to him simply as trust funds, which he is called upon to administer, and strictly bound as a matter of duty to administer in the manner which, in his judgment, is best calculated to provide the most beneficial results for the community—the man of wealth thus becoming the mere trustee and agent for his poorer brethren."

Carnegie endowed colleges, hospitals, and other institutions, but his aid in establishing hundreds of free public libraries open to all in towns and cities throughout the United States was perhaps his most beneficial work. Carnegie funds usually erected the building and the town provided the site and maintenance.

Photo: Library of Congress

Chautauqua–

A Great Educational and Cultural Movement

During the summer of 1874 a young minister conducted training sessions for Sunday School teachers on the banks of Lake Chautauqua in New York. From this modest beginning grew an educational and cultural movement that swept the nation and for fifty years helped quench throughout the land a thirst for good music, stage plays, lectures, and a wide variety of theatrical performances.

Starting in the spring, a troupe composed of such headline attractions as William Jennings Bryan, Madame Schumann-Heink, the Swiss Bell Ringers, a noted explorer and sundry minor acts would tour the country until fall, presenting their program in a large tent such as those used by a circus. Advance agents made financial arrangements and worked out other details with the town's most cultured, refined, wealthy, and morally pure citizens who sponsored a day or a week of Chautauqua. Around the "Big Top"

were smaller tents occupied by families who had traveled a long distance to spend an exhilarating week seeing magical tricks, listening to famous lecturers, hearing classical music and watching plays. The all-time favorite lecture was "Acres of Diamonds" given more than 6,000 times by Dr. Russell H. Conwell. His theme was that almost anyone can become wealthy and successful if he applies himself and especially if he resists the lure of green pastures and concentrates on the "acres of diamonds" lying at his feet.

Chautauqua came to an end during the 1920's, when movies, radio, good roads and automobiles made it possible to enjoy good entertainment every day instead of once a year in the stifling heat of a tent pitched in a grove on the edge of town.

Photo: From the Judge Ben B. Lindsey Collection

"Twilight on the Trail"

The strength of character and native intelligence of the pioneer woman is exemplified in this picture of a modern-day mountaineer lady. During her lifetime she saw the frontier disappear and the miracles of the machine age change a way of life that had long seemed changeless.

Photo: Hugh Morton

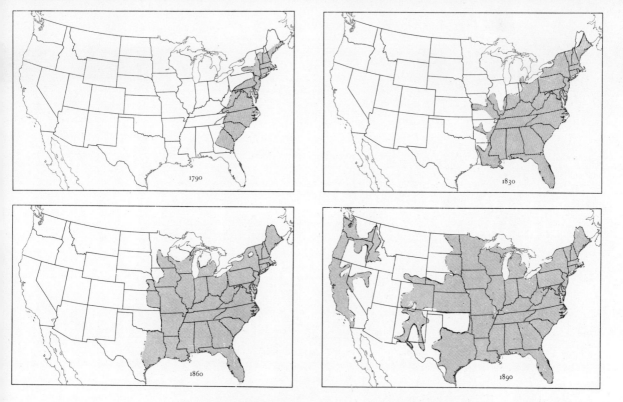

The Shifting Lines of the Frontier
1790–1890

By 1890, the wavering line of the frontier, indicating a population of two persons per square mile or more, had pushed west from the Atlantic to the Rocky Mountains, joining a similar line that had crept slowly from the Pacific coast east to the Rockies.

There remained pockets of unsettled land, but in a real sense the frontier was no more. Nearly three hundred years had come and gone since the first permanent settlement at Jamestown, Virginia, but at last the period of pioneering was ending.

Density of Population
1890

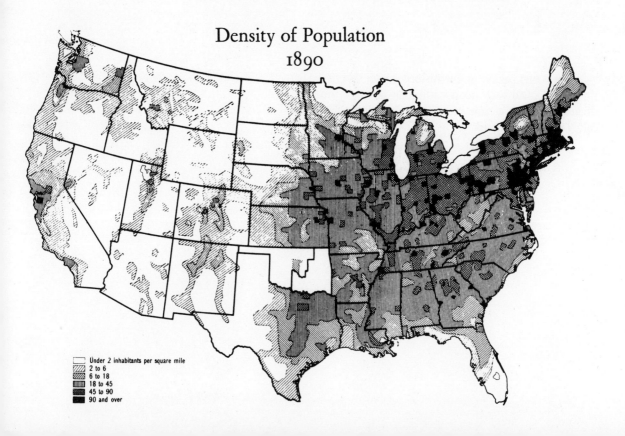

Under 2 inhabitants per square mile
2 to 6
6 to 18
18 to 45
45 to 90
90 and over

Photo: Library of Congress

There is one period in our history which everyone since has looked back upon with great nostalgia and dreamed of it as a time of peace and pleasure. It is called the Gay Nineties.

THE LONG BEGINNING ENDS

Saratoga Springs, N.Y., during the Gay Nineties

The decade 1890–1900 has been labeled the "Gay Nineties" not because it was actually gay but because, compared to all that had gone before, it appeared to be a particularly happy period. The reasons are easy to find. By 1890, the frontier was gone, Indians were subdued, peace, prosperity, and plenty seemed assured forever, wonderful new inventions and scientific developments were almost daily events, and for the first time large numbers of people had the leisure and money to indulge themselves in pleasurable pursuits. These included playing golf, lawn tennis, and croquet, bicycling, boating, going on vacation trips, attending sports events, and dining at good restaurants. The new-found freedom for women gave all these pastimes an exhilaration not previously present. Young women whose mothers had braved the wilds to improve their lot were not to be dissuaded by snide remarks from exploiting the opportunities for business employment and the "better things in life." Men were getting soft anyhow. In 1875 baseball catchers started wearing masks and, ten years later, chest protectors. That was the same year men began having a crease put in their trousers. Further, the slates of school children had a border of soft felt padding to muffle noise. A safety catch was required by law on elevators in public buildings. Some women gave up riding horses sidesaddle and redesigned their clothes to provide greater freedom of movement. Home decoration became a matter of much consideration. Cut glass was a prime necessity until the automobile came along to absorb surplus funds.

More and more people took time off from work for vacations at the beach or other resort areas. Among the most famous was the spa at Saratoga Springs, New York, where well-to-do patrons put up at the U.S. Hotel (opposite) or the Grand Union Hotel further down the block. Strolling the tree-shaded streets, lounging at the mineral springs, watching the races, attending costume balls, and gambling in the casinos made the vacationer feel that he was living the life of European royalty. The long beginning was over. The young nation had survived a turbulent youth, reached a virile young manhood, and was set to move forward with an accumulation of knowledge and skills to be put to work turning out a galaxy of things for the home, farm, and factory that would make life easier and better for everybody. It didn't quite work out that way, but that was the way it looked during the Gay Nineties.

Lumbering Operations in the Old Days

An insatiable demand for lumber arose during the late years of the nineteenth century to supply a resurgent Chicago, for building homes throughout the Midwest where brick and stone were scarce and expensive, and for railroad ties, freight cars, mine props, and a hundred other purposes. This demand was met by exploiting the vast, virgin forests of white pine in the nearby Great Lakes states. The man with the ax, aided by new and improved timber-cutting machinery, tore into age-old stands of magnificent trees and within short years laid them low.

Photo: U.S. Forest Service

Huge Raft in the Pacific Northwest

Meanwhile the Pacific Northwest was humming with activity as forests yielded millions of board feet of timber and places like Seattle became great ports with ships in the harbor from all over the world and a brisk trade developing with the Orient. Rafts like this one (below) being towed through Deception Pass in Washington on its way to southern California contained more than two million board feet of fir, cedar, and hemlock.

Photo: USDA by Harms

Stump Fences

When stump-pulling equipment was perfected, it became customary, especially in the Great Lakes states, to move the stumps to one side of a field, where they were laid side by side to form a fence.

Valley Agriculture in the Great West

Throughout the mountainous areas of the West a valley agriculture developed where soils were suitable and rainfall adequate for raising crops or where water from sparkling streams fed by the melted snow of the mountain ranges could be used for irrigation. Grain was grown here in this clearing in the verdant Hood River Valley, in Oregon, which in more recent years has become famed for its production of fruit.

Mining Coal
in Pennsylvania

Among the marvelous, strange, and weird things that Marco Polo related seeing in China around A.D. 1200 was the burning of "black rocks" to provide heat. No one paid much attention to his yarns. But when the industrial revolution came, coal was the fuel which stoked its fires and made possible the development of the machine age. Formed of vegetation that flourished thousands of years ago and was then buried deep in the ground when violent contortions shifted the earth's surface, coal deposits are found in more than half of the states. Bituminous coal, containing some 60 per cent of carbon, is the most common.

The coal mines of Pennsylvania within a few short years changed the state from being predominantly agricultural to predominantly industrial. Since 1900, West Virginia has produced over five billion tons of bituminous coal. More than five hundred million tons of coal are produced annually to meet the needs of a nation which in the 1890's was continuing an industrial upsurge that had started during the Civil War.

Coal and Iron Ore Create Giant Steel Industry

The Bessemer process, developed in England just prior to our Civil War, converted cast iron into steel by burning out the impurities with air. Utilizing the coal, ore, and limestone readily available, and adapting the Bessemer method, Pittsburgh rapidly developed into the industrial center of America during the decades following the Civil War. By 1890 there was a tremendous demand for steel for railroad rails, locomotives, ships, bridges, wire fences, and many other uses. In 1884 the Home Insurance Company of Chicago, Illinois, put up an office building based on an entirely new type of construction. Instead of brick walls supporting the entire weight of the building, a cast-iron and steel skeleton of supports and cross beams was built and masonry walls were put up around it. This ten-story building, the first "skyscraper," is still standing. Soon, steel replaced iron in construction of the framework. With the base solidly attached to bedrock and with the walls relieved of the dead weight of the entire building, there is hardly any limit to the height skyscrapers can be built. The Empire State Building has 102 stories and a height of 1,250 feet.

218

Mesabi Iron Ore Range in Minnesota

As the iron ore deposits that had made Pittsburgh an industrial giant began to show signs of depletion, a huge new field of ore was opened in northern Minnesota. The Mesabi Range, as it is called, contained an apparently inexhaustible supply of ore so close to the surface that ditch-digging equipment could mine the ore from open pits. The principal problem was to utilize ore so far removed from the coal needed to convert it into steel. Transporting ore a thousand miles and more by railroad was not economically feasible, but, fortunately, after a rail haul of about a hundred miles the ore could be put on boats plying the Great Lakes that would deposit it at ports within a hundred miles of Pittsburgh. Despite the inconvenience and cost of loading and unloading six times, this was more economical than hauling twice as much coal west to the Mesabi Range, since it requires two tons of coal to reduce one ton of ore. Further, the principal markets for steel were east of Pittsburgh, hence moving the ore east from Minnesota was in the direction of its ultimate destination. An additional factor were the established plants for production of steel in the Pittsburgh area, supplied already with machinery and equipment, managerial ability, skilled labor supply, capital, and transportation.

Photo: National Archives

Apostolic Clock in Pennsylvania

This elaborately carved and intricately designed clock, completed in 1878 by John Feister of Lancaster County, Pennsylvania, required eleven years to make. In the upper section of the clock animated figures of the Apostles, Judas, Satan, Justice and others perform complex maneuvers as they enact scenes from the Bible each quarter hour. This marvelous clock is a type of hand-created object seldom seen in these times, since the skill and imagination required is now used to design and build the labor saving and efficient machinery essential in mass production of innumerable items.

Photo: Community Information Centre, Department of the Hershey Estates

"Return from America" by F. Hiddeman

This painting tells its own story. It was popular in the late nineteenth century, when golden opportunities in the New World across the sea were being energetically extolled throughout Europe.

Courtesy E. B. Crocker Art Gallery

Court of Honor, Columbian Exposition, Chicago, 1893

In Chicago in 1893, the four hundredth anniversary of the landing of Columbus was celebrated, a year late but nevertheless in a spectacular and epochal manner. It would be difficult to name a phase of American life that was not affected by the great exposition and its vast array of exhibits of the arts and sciences which were viewed by over twenty-seven million visitors. The "Court of Honor" built for the Exposition inspired the architecture of the Federal Triangle and other government buildings in Washington, D.C.

Livestock shows, agricultural displays and industrial exhibitions have played an important part in the development of this country, stimulating interest in new inventions and better ways of accomplishing old tasks. State and county fairs have long been annual affairs with contestants competing for prizes in a wide range of contests including canning pickles, raising vegetables, fruits, field crops, and livestock, racing by horse and auto and on foot, all capped, of course, by a beauty contest. The throngs that visited the Columbian Exposition in 1893 had visible evidence that the United States at long last was passing "from the gristle to the solid bone of manhood."

Photo: National Archives

Lafayette Square Opera House, Washington, D.C.

Additional evidence of the "new culture" was the appearance in most cities throughout the country of opera houses, which served for all kinds of stage productions and occasionally for the presentation of an opera by a traveling troupe. One such opera house was on Lafayette Square in Washington, D.C., close to the White House. It opened on the night of September 30, 1895, with Lillian Russell appearing in *The Tzigane* (Gypsy), a Russian comic opera in three acts. This was followed by such old favorites as *Belle of New York, The Old Homestead,* and *Heart of Maryland,* with casts including John Drew, E. H. Sothern, Richard Mansfield, DeWolf Hopper, Julia Marlowe, E. S. Willard, Maude Adams, May Irwin, and other famous stars. Many Americans have never really enjoyed opera, served to them in a foreign language in a stuffed-shirt atmosphere which seemed strictly phony to a forthright and unpretentious people. Lighter plays and comedies were popular, however, until the moving pictures came along. However, a few opera stars have gained widespread personal popularity, notably Enrico Caruso and Madame Schumann-Heink.

Photo: District of Columbia Historical Society

Henry Ford in his First Automobile, 1896

For over a hundred years, at home and abroad, mechanics had experimented with various means of motive power for replacing horses. Steam, electricity, and gasoline were not considered of much practical significance. Then, in 1896, a thirty-three-year-old farmer's son named Henry Ford took off in a curious-looking contraption powered by a tiny gasoline engine that the young mechanic had built in the woodshed back of his home. It was not the first gasoline horseless carriage and perhaps not even the best one, but coupled to the productive genius of Henry Ford it was destined to remake the face of the earth. In 1895 there were only four registered motor vehicles in the United States. Five years later there were eight thousand and at mid-century nearly fifty million.

Photo: Henry Ford Museum, Dearborn, Michigan

The Cotton Boll Weevil Invades the United States

It was a bad day for American cotton farmers when, during the 1890's, a tiny insect no more than a quarter of an inch long, crossed the border from Mexico and attacked cotton bolls. Since a pair of these vicious pests can produce twelve million progeny from spring to fall, it was only a short time before cotton fields were seriously infected. Traveling twenty-five to fifty miles a year, the boll weevil spread throughout the cotton kingdom and season after season caused millions of dollars in damage. A half century later, despite scientific countermeasures, the boll weevil in South Carolina alone inflicted losses estimated at fifty-five million dollars.

Photo: Clemson Agricultural College Extension Service

Rural Carrier on his Route at Crawfordsville, Indiana

City folks had become accustomed to having mail delivered to their doors morning and afternoon for many years. But it was not until 1896 that Congress passed the Rural Free Mail Delivery Act. Three years later, when this picture was taken, there were four hundred and twelve routes involving 8,929 miles of travel to serve approximately sixty thousand families; by mid-century, a network of rural mail routes throughout the nation aggregated over a million and a half miles. Daily mail service to isolated farms played an important part in bringing town and country closer together.

As the fourth century after Columbus drew to a close, it was clear that the old days of good free land, unlimited resources, and emphasis on agriculture were over and that henceforth problems of an urban population would take precedence. The 1847 potato famine in Ireland, religious persecution, aversion to military service, and economic "hard times" abroad, coupled with the rapid spread of the mechanical revo-

lution in the United States and glowing accounts of opportunities for all in America, had brought a tremendous increase in immigration. The nation which had been an infant in 1800 with an area of only 892,000 square miles and a population of five million had grown in one momentous century to an area of 3,027,000 square miles and a population of seventy-six million.

Photo: U.S. Post Office Department

VII. THE FIFTH HUNDRED YEARS—1900-

GROWING UP—TRANSITION BETWEEN WORLD WARS—SOME POST WAR REGIONAL PATTERNS—THE NORTH: FAMILY-SIZE FARMS, MANUFACTURING, COMMERCE AND THE MELTING POT—THE SOUTH: PLANTATIONS, TIMBER, CITRUS, SUNSHINE AND NEW INDUSTRIES—THE WEST: CATTLE RANCHES, SCENERY, MINING, MOVIES AND WIDE OPEN SPACES

Vigorous Theodore Roosevelt, who became President in 1901 when President McKinley was killed, typified the transition period in which he lived. He combined the hunter and horseman of the old frontier, the conservationist and social reformer of the new industrialism, and the enlightened internationalist of the World War I period. The Spanish-American War left the United States uncertain what to do about the Philippines but certain that it wanted no overseas colonies. In 1912, New Mexico and Arizona were admitted into the Union, becoming numbers 47 and 48 respectively, thus rounding out the number of continental states, although Texas has the right, if she so chooses, to sub-divide and become five states.

The out-break of war in Europe in 1914 seemed a matter of little concern to Americans. The desire was only for peace, prosperity and more of President Wilson's "New Freedom." Some local disturbances occurred along the Mexican border, and Germans were irritating Americans, but Woodrow Wilson was doing some "watchful waiting" in the White House. The forgetful thought that war would not come to America. Finally the war in Europe involved the United States just as it had been involved in previous European wars. At the end of the war President Wilson sponsored a League of Nations which he hoped would insure peace for the world. The plan was repudiated by the U. S. Senate. Post-war prosperity was followed by the Great Depression which played its part in furthering World War II. Vigorous efforts were made to aid farmers, industrial workers and raise the standard of living of all during Franklin Roosevelt's administration.

When war drums began to throb again in Europe, the people of the United States of America were determined that *this* time they would positively stay out of the fight. "Let them come over here and we'll knock 'em back in the water" was the attitude of many, but it was no use, for eventually the United States was caught in its ninth world-wide conflict. More than 450,000 Americans were killed in the War and between 1940 and 1945 the public debt increased from $61 billion to $226 billion. Approximately eighty-five cents of each tax dollar goes for wars, past, present, or prospective, a strange situation for a nation which for 150 years has tried to avoid wars and has made no attempt to build an overseas empire.

When the Union Station in Washington, D. C. was completed in 1907, it was large enough to hold the entire Army, Navy, and Marine Corps of the United States. That was true in 1907, it was true in 1914 when World War I broke out in Europe; it was true in 1933 when Hitler came to power in Germany; and it was true in 1939 when World War II began. Because this country desired peace, its armed forces were kept to a mere handful, but this desire was interpreted as weakness and an unwillingness to fight regardless of what happened. Let the record speak for itself. It is to be hoped that no aggressor ever again is misled by our "easy going" attitude.

Following World War II, industrial production soared to unbelievable heights, providing better housing, automobiles, and household equipment such as television, refrigerators, dish washers, and furnaces, in brief a higher standard of living for everybody. More people were church members than ever before, and any project designed to achieve better relations between people received enthusiastic supporters. International cooperation and technical assistance spearheaded by President Truman's Point Four Program helped relieve war torn areas and develop latent resources throughout the Free World. The American Dream of a better material, social, and spiritual life for all people seemed near at hand. However, the World had a new and somber worry—the atom bomb, its hideous offspring, the hydrogen bomb, and the satellite station—the future of which for good or evil was shrouded in the fogs of the future. But it was unmistakable that these fearful instruments had created a world in which there is no place to hide.

President Theodore Roosevelt and Gifford Pinchot

"Teddy" Roosevelt and Gifford Pinchot, two great fighters in early battles for conservation of our natural resources, talk things over aboard the *Mississippi* in 1907 on a Potomac River cruise.

Photo: U.S. Forest Service

First Motor-powered Flight of Man

In 1903 this picture was taken at Kitty Hawk, North Carolina, of one of the Wright brothers stretched out on a crude airplane with which he was making man's first successful motor-powered flight. This spectacular event ushered in a new era, the full significance of which can even yet be only guessed. In addition to military uses and passenger service, the airplane has been used to spray orchards, dust cotton, seed pastures, and plant rice, for rapid transport of perishables to market, and in efforts to create precipitation when and where needed.

Orville and Wilbur Wright, sons of a preacher, made their living operating a small bicycle shop, never attended college, and pursued efforts to fly in spite of the opposition of scientists and ridicule from the public.

Photo: North Carolina Department of Conservation and Development

Roosevelt Dam in Arizona

In the West beyond the twenty-inch rainfall line which bisects the Dakotas, Nebraska, Kansas, Oklahoma, and Texas crops can be grown with reasonable certainty only by irrigation. However, the development of an irrigation system is a mammoth and complex undertaking requiring much money and the coordinated effort of a large number of farmers, ditch operators, and others strung out over long distances. Progress, therefore, was slow until the decade 1870–80, at the end of which about a million acres of farm land were being irrigated. From 1880–90 there was great activity in building privately financed irrigation projects. The Census of 1890 revealed 3,632,000 acres under irrigation on 54,000 farms. In 1902 the Federal Bureau of Reclamation was founded and in the next fifty years invested over two billion dollars in irrigation projects having over four million kilowatts of hydroelectric generating capacity, 6,400 miles of transmission lines, and water for more than six million acres of productive land. Impressive as these figures are, they actually indicate the relatively tiny amount of land under irrigation. Even if all currently proposed projects were put into operation, irrigated areas would be merely a few scattered oases in a vast land of mountains and deserts.

The Roosevelt Dam in Arizona, which went into operation in 1911, was the first great dam constructed by the government. It has been followed by many others since then.

Photo: USDA. by Berlyn Brixner

A Salesman Visits Farm Homes

During horse and buggy days, outfits such as the one above were a common sight throughout rural America as itinerant salesmen traveled from farm to farm, dispensing, along with home remedies, extracts, and flavors, household necessities and livestock feed supplements, a variety of extra services ranging from advice on cooking, baking, care of furniture, and the like to the most up-to-date information from state universities on farm management, insect control, and livestock feeding. These enterprising "drummers" spread knowledge of new gadgets and household appliances into remote areas, thus creating demand where none had existed before and helping to create and maintain the great and complex merchandising system which has done so much to raise the standard of living of American rural communities. Today, neat panel trucks, pickup trucks, and station wagons have replaced the horse-drawn vehicles of yesteryear, but the Watkins Products man and representatives of similar concerns still roam the countryside and many cover the same locality and call on the same families that they have visited for two generations or more.

Photo: Courtesy the J. R. Watkins Company

The 1902 Sears, Roebuck Catalogue

Sears, Roebuck and Company, the largest merchandising concern in the United States, got its start in North Redwood, Minnesota, in 1886 as a mail-order house. With the extension of free mail service to rural areas throughout the country, the company, selling a wide variety of articles of good quality which were reasonably priced and guaranteed, soon became a household name. Its catalogue, with a multitude of enticing articles attractively presented, was an endless source of pleasure to the entire family. The above composite picture was made up from items advertised on four of the more than a thousand pages in the 1902 catalogue. Present-day catalogues now list over a hundred thousand different items.

Photo: Sears, Roebuck and Company

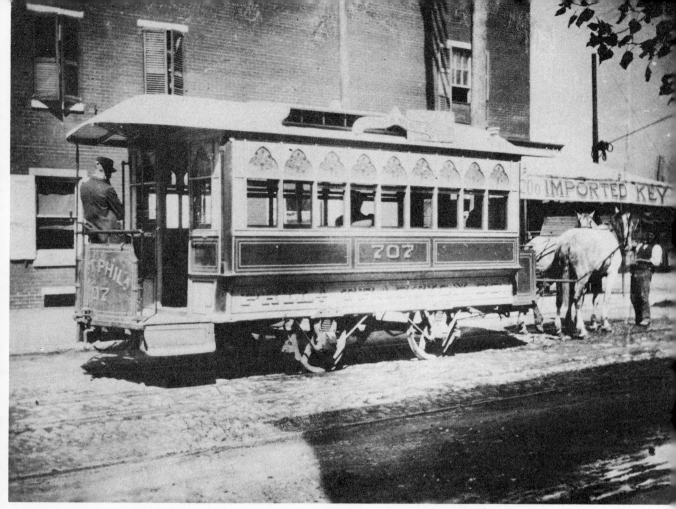

A Horse-Drawn Streetcar

Horse-drawn streetcars were a familiar sight in larger American towns and cities until the first decade of the twentieth century.

Photo: Library of Congress

The Village Blacksmith

The blacksmith was a personage of importance throughout the long period that the horse was the principal source of motive power. Shoeing horses was a constant and recurring need, and making vehicles and repairing harness, wagons, carts, buggies, and machinery of all sorts made the blacksmith shop a center of activity. Henry Wadsworth Longfellow's poem "The Village Blacksmith," eulogizing the smithy, is indicative of the high standing which skilled labor and the honest workman have always had in this country. A few shops remain where one can see "the flaming forge" and "hear the bellows roar."

Photo: USDA by Forsythe

233

An Independently Owned Store

The period between the Spanish American War (1898) and America's entry into World War I (1917) was the heyday of the individually owned general store, such as this one, to be found in every village and town where ladies, dressed in long skirts and large, festooned hats, shopped for groceries, dishes, and household furnishings, including oil lamps of curious design and hand-painted shades. Such stores, with their canned fruit, vegetables, and salmon and neat pasteboard packages, were a long step forward from the old-time picturesque but unsanitary store with its open cracker barrel and bulk handling of food products.

Photo: Wyoming State Historical Department

Listening in on a Party Line

The telephone, invented by the Scottish emigrant Alexander Graham Bell in 1876, was in general use in towns and cities throughout the country by 1900 and by 1920 in many rural areas. The rural telephone, occasionally used for business calls or to summon a doctor or undertaker, served the farm family, especially the women, as radio, television, bridge club, and newspaper. Several families on the same line could listen in on each other's conversations and thus keep up with neighborhood affairs. Listening in, or "piking" as it was called in some communities, was a recognized practice, carried no implication of "snooping," and still continues as more and more farms acquire telephone service.

Photo: Rural Electrification Administration

A Firetrap Takes 146 Lives

On March 25, 1911, the Triangle Waist Company in New York City was destroyed by fire, and 146 workers, many of them women and girls, lost their lives. Tragedy though it was, this shocking disaster sparked a drive that is still continuing throughout the nation to improve all aspects of working conditions, including sanitation, accident prevention, lighting, length of work day, wage rates, child labor, avoidance of poisoning and disease, elimination of fire hazards, and other menaces to the safety and welfare of workers. The 1911 session of the New York State Legislature, of which Franklin D. Roosevelt,

Alfred E. Smith, and Robert F. Wagner were members, took the lead in investigating conditions in factories, mines, and shops, passing remedial legislation, and enforcing safety laws and regulations. In the forefront of the fight to improve working conditions were many people later nationally prominent: Frances Perkins, Henry L. Stimson, William G. McAdoo, Henry Morgenthau, and Samuel Gompers.

Photo: International Ladies' Garment Workers' Union

"American Gothic"

This famous painting by Grant Wood depicts better than words could the character and way of life of the farm folk of this nation. Plain, simple clothes, a stern visage with only a hint of deep-seated humor, the sturdy strength and serious cast of rugged faces all reflect the plain living, high thinking, conscientious attention to duty, and energetic activity characteristic of people of the "Bible belt." For such as these the words "work for the night is coming" are a way of life.

Photo: Courtesy of the Art Institute of Chicago

The Famous Model T Ford

Models of the first Ford car put out in 1896 followed in rapid succession until the Model T, a light, low-priced (about $500), high-wheeled car designed for rough, unpaved roads, emerged in 1908. There were many jokes about the "Tin Lizzie," but during the next nineteen years more than fifteen million Fords were put on the road. The demand for new cars brought about revolutionary new production methods, especially the development in 1913 of assembly-line production which made it possible to put together a car like the one pictured below in eighty-three minutes rather than in twelve and a half hours as had previously been required. This easy-to-operate, simple-to-repair, sturdy, low-priced car along with other makes on the market created allied industries to produce parts and accessories, provided a market for vast new oil discoveries, forced the building of good roads in town and country, raised wage scales, and, in brief, changed the life of a nation. In 1908 there were more than three hundred different makes of American automobiles, of which less than a dozen are now being produced.

Photo: Smithsonian Institution

The PENALTY OF LEADERSHIP

IN every field of human endeavor, he that is first must perpetually live in the white light of publicity. ¶Whether the leadership be vested in a man or in a manufactured product, emulation and envy are ever at work. ¶In art, in literature, in music, in industry, the reward and the punishment are always the same. ¶The reward is widespread recognition; the punishment, fierce denial and detraction. ¶When a man's work becomes a standard for the whole world, it also becomes a target for the shafts of the envious few. ¶If his work be merely mediocre, he will be left severely alone—if he achieve a masterpiece, it will set a million tongues a-wagging. ¶Jealousy does not protrude its forked tongue at the artist who produces a commonplace painting. ¶Whatsoever you write, or paint, or play, or sing, or build, no one will strive to surpass, or to slander you, unless your work be stamped with the seal of genius. ¶Long, long after a great work or a good work has been done, those who are disappointed or envious continue to cry out that it can not be done. ¶Spiteful little voices in the domain of art were raised against our own Whistler as a mountebank, long after the big world had acclaimed him its greatest artistic genius. ¶Multitudes flocked to Bayreuth to worship at the musical shrine of Wagner, while the little group of those whom he had dethroned and displaced argued angrily that he was no musician at all. ¶The little world continued to protest that Fulton could never build a steamboat, while the big world flocked to the river banks to see his boat steam by. ¶The leader is assailed because he is a leader, and the effort to equal him is merely added proof of that leadership. ¶Failing to equal or to excel, the follower seeks to depreciate and to destroy—but only confirms once more the superiority of that which he strives to supplant. ¶There is nothing new in this. ¶It is as old as the world and as old as the human passions—envy, fear, greed, ambition, and the desire to surpass. ¶And it all avails nothing. ¶If the leader truly leads, he remains—the leader. ¶Master-poet, master-painter, master-workman, each in his turn is assailed, and each holds his laurels through the ages. ¶That which is good or great makes itself known, no matter how loud the clamor of denial. ¶That which deserves to live—lives.

Cadillac Motor Car Co. Detroit, Mich.

A Famous Advertisement

Convinced that "it pays to advertise," the automobile industry early spent huge sums for advertising. It has put many millions into advertising in newspapers, magazines, on radio and television, for sales "literature," contest prizes and special features of every sort. Whether all this outlay was, and is, necessary to achieve and maintain the success of the motorcar may be debatable but it is a dynamic enterprise.

One of the cleverest and most effective advertisements ever printed was "The Penalty of Leadership," reproduced above, which never once mentioned the product it was selling—the Cadillac car.

Reprinted with permission of the Saturday Evening Post *and the Cadillac Division of General Motors Corporation*

Rural Roads in Early Days of the Automobile

In cities, prior to the First World War, principal streets had long been paved with brick, and sprinkling dirt streets with water to settle the dust and soaking them with crude oil were also common practices. Beyond city limits, however, were few improvements and often, because of rain or snow, roads were practically impassable by automobile. Motorists' eager urge to "go places" was continually hampered by the hazards and frustrations of travel on narrow, winding, unsurfaced roads designed for horse-drawn vehicles and by a lack of uniformity in maintenance of roads by different states and even counties. As the number of automobiles rapidly increased, the clamor for better roads compelled county, state, and national governments to undertake extensive road-building programs which are still in progress. The present road system is considered inadequate for future needs.

Photo: American Automobile Association

One of the First County Agricultural Agents

Land-grant colleges provided expert training for agricultural specialists, and experiment stations tested many new plants and farm practices. But the ordinary farmer did not reap the full benefit of this new knowledge until the cooperative Agricultural Extension Service was established in 1914. J. A. Evans, one of the first county agents, is making his round of visits to farms where his advice, like that of his associates, soon became highly regarded.

Photo: U.S. Extension Service

William S. Hart Starred in the Silent Movies

In 1839 a Frenchman, Daguerre, and an Englishman, Talbot, developed methods for making good pictures in a matter of a few minutes; not quite fifty years later the Reverend Hannibal Goodwin and George Eastman discovered a method of making celluloid film; in 1893 Thomas Edison invented the kinetoscope, or box viewer, which an Englishman converted to a projector with a series of small pictures moved rapidly in sequence to denote motion. The first actual motion-picture theater was opened in 1902 in Los Angeles, and shortly most towns had a "nickelodeon" where for a nickel a one-reel silent film of the pie-throwing type could be seen. The first movie to tell a story was *The Great Train Robbery* in 1905. A dozen years of movie progress brought D. W. Griffith's great success, *The Birth of a Nation,* followed by rapid improvements in which sound was combined with pictures in 1927 and color added about a

decade later. Hollywood became the center of the movie industry, primarily because of its climate and scenery.

An old Hollywood maxim says, "When you *must* produce a money-making movie, make a Western." In 1902 Owen Wister, an Eastern man with a fondness for Wyoming, wrote *The Virginian* in which he included practically all the ingredients found in every Western since then; that is, a tall, handsome, soft-spoken hero who rides a good horse, has a run-in with a despicable character in a saloon, gets into trouble with cattle rustlers, fights a gun duel in the streets of a cow town, and marries the beautiful schoolteacher from the East. The list of male stars who have played *The Virginian* includes Gary Cooper, Joel McCrea, and various others. William S. Hart, shown above in a typical pose, was an early movie star.

Photo: Library of Congress

The Greatest Mother in the World

The First World War meant many things to many institutions but to the American Red Cross it meant an opportunity to demonstrate to the world its ability to serve mankind. Wherever there were misery, grief, hardship, pain, sickness, loneliness, and worry, there also was the Red Cross. Nursing service, canteens, first aid, convalescent care, refugee relief, war prisoner service, hospital supervision, and home medical assistance are conspicuous activities carried on by the Red Cross at home and abroad. The people of the United States were slow to participate fully in the International Red Cross because of fear of "foreign entanglements," but since World War I, the service has been given wholehearted support throughout the nation. Many other organizations have contributed to the relief and rehabilitation of soldiers, sailors, and civilians: the Salvation Army, Y.M.C.A., Knights of Columbus, etc.

Photo: American Red Cross

The GREATEST MOTHER *in the* WORLD

End of an Era, 1920

Secretary of Agriculture, David F. Houston, who served from 1913 to 1920, was the last of the "horse and buggy" secretaries, but the end of his term in office marked other and far more important changes. The conversion from carriage to automobile coincided with momentous facts not fully appreciated at the time. This country was developed on borrowed money, most of it from Europe, but now the debts had been paid and the United States had changed from being a debtor to a creditor nation. The principal agricultural problem was no longer production but marketing. The 250-year struggle to clear the forests and to get people onto the land followed by fifty years of unrelenting search for new and better plants and animals and improved farm practices had re-

sulted in a prodigious outpouring of agricultural commodities. During World War I, industrial facilities had been expanded tremendously. After the Armistice, a large part of industry was converted to peacetime production. Europe was going through an agonizing period of reconstruction, Russia was in the grips of a revolution, the Far East was struggling with age-old problems, but the United States seemed on its way "back to normalcy."

Photo: USDA

Industry and Agriculture Are Dependent on Each Other

By 1920, only one person in four gainfully employed was engaged in agriculture, and for the first time less than half the population lived in rural communities. However, the interdependence of farm and nonfarm segments is indicated here by such industrial products as the motor truck and steam engine being used to provide wheat needed for factory workers' bread. The collapse of the wartime agricultural prosperity brought hard times to farmers long before the stock market crash of 1929 heralded the industrial depression. Mechanization of methods used in agricultural production, harvesting, and marketing continued to increase and provided employment for factory workers in the plants of implement manufacturers.

Photo: USDA by McManigal

A Home Demonstration Agent Heads for the Hills

Improvement in farming methods and increased yields brought with them a desire of farm women to learn new ways of doing old tasks. College-trained home demonstration agents brought to farm women the "know-how" developed in colleges which made rural homes more attractive and housework easier. It was the efforts of home demonstration agents like Miss Elizabeth Scoville, with her equipment slung over her shoulder, riding horseback over the hills and mountains of her isolated district during the 1920's, which, as a foreign visitor once pointed out, "makes it impossible to tell a country girl from a city girl."

Photo: USDA

Transition from "Jolt Wagon" to "Flivver"

Means of transportation changed radically as the automobile came into general use and bad roads were converted to good highways. A farmer, his wife, and their eight children arrive at a community club meeting in a wagon—a form of transportation seldom seen now but common a few years ago. The transition from "jolt wagon" to "flivver" proceeded rapidly and by mid-century was nearly complete.

Photo: Tennessee Extension Service

Stern Paddle and Diesel Barge

This old and exhausted stern paddle wheel of some bygone river boat highlights the old and new, as a modern tow in the background pushes a line of barges upstream. The largest of the old-time steamboats carried only two to three hundred tons of freight, whereas a single modern barge can carry as much as four thousand tons. By hooking barges together, tremendous loads can be moved easily and swiftly. River traffic of today does not have the romantic appeal of yesteryear, but the tonnage involved is many times that of old steamboat days.

Photo: Kentucky State Division of Publicity

The Crystal Radio Set

The initial discovery in 1893 by the nineteen-year-old Italian youth, Marconi, that messages can be transmitted via air waves without wires opened a new world which is still being explored. In the early 1920's when this picture was taken, the crystal radio set was causing excitement and much loss of sleep throughout the land as old and young listened over earphones to feeble broadcasting stations. In 1923, Woodrow Wilson made a radio talk to the nation, the first ex-President to speak over radio. Rapid progress was made, and within a decade radios were in nearly every home. The Dempsey-Tunney prize fights; Wayne King's dreamy waltzes; Will Rogers' humor, football games described by Graham McNamee, "Amos and Andy," and the crooning of Bing Crosby were among the highlights of early days of radio. Near the close of the decade Al Jolson made the first talking movie, *The Jazz Singer,* in which sound and motion were synchronized.

Photo: National Archives

A Monument to the Boll Weevil

Despite tremendous losses suffered annually from boll weevils, at least one Southern community thought it profited by their activities. In Enterprise, Alabama, can be seen the only monument in the world erected in honor of an insect pest, the boll weevil, deadly enemy of cotton. The farmers of that community had raised cotton year in and year out and always there was a battle with this fierce and persistent foe. Finally the ravages of the boll weevil forced the farmers to try something other than cotton and they experimented with growing peanuts. The results were amazing and soon the community was thriving again. Out of gratitude to the boll weevil, for forcing them to try something besides cotton, citizens erected a monument on the main street of Enterprise.

Photo: by Chesnut—Alabama Polytechnic Institute

Development of the Chain Store and Supermarket

During the 1920's the chain store, which had become a familiar institution through such far-flung merchandising concerns as the F. W. Woolworth Co., began to spread into many fields, including the grocery business. Because of savings accomplished through large-scale buying, efficient handling, and other methods, chain stores can usually undersell the locally owned store. They have taken over the bulk of retail food distributing. "Serve yourself and pay as you leave" supermarkets such as this one carry a great variety of food products and are operated by trained managers hired by a corporation with hundreds of similar stores throughout the nation.

Installment buying in which a small down payment is required and the remainder of the purchase price is paid regularly in monthly or other periodic installments became very popular. "Easy to pay" plans made it seem easy to buy automobiles, washing machines, furniture, clothes, equipment, and other desirable articles.

Photo: Bert Giles, Raleigh, N. C.

The Decline of the Horse

Ironically, just as better roads, rubber tires, and other improvements were making life easier for horses and mules, the automobile, motor truck, and tractor came along to displace them. The drastic reduction in the number of horses and mules to less than a fourth of the 1915 peak of twenty-six million head has freed for food production and for other purposes more than seventy-five million acres of cropland formerly used to produce feed for workstock.

Photo: USDA by Forsythe

Auto Racing Helps Improve Automobiles

Development of the automobile has been furthered by lessons learned from auto racing, especially in Indiana at the Indianapolis Motor Speedway. Many modern-day features of the automobile received their most grueling tests during the annual 500-mile auto race which is often witnessed by more than a hundred thousand spectators. Built in 1909 as a testing ground for automobiles, the dirt track caused accidents from the outset and soon was provided with a paved surface for which more than three million bricks were used. The track has since been surfaced with asphalt.

The winner of the first 500-mile Indianapolis Speedway race in 1911 averaged 74.59 miles an hour; forty years later the winner averaged 125.24 miles per hour. Although more widely known for his exploits as an aviator, Captain Eddie Rickenbacker gained his earliest fame as a racer at the Indianapolis Speedway. The 2½-mile course is 50 feet wide, the front and back stretches are each 3,300 feet, the north and south ends are each 660 feet, and the four turns are each 1,320 feet long.

Photo: by O'Dell & Shields, Indianapolis Chamber of Commerce

Paved Roads and Electricity Make for Better Living

A welcome sight to rural people everywhere is that of men stringing lines to carry electricity to farm communities. Better lights are helpful, but the greatest boon is the electric motor used to run milking machines, power tools, water pumps, feed grinders, and washing machines. Over 90 per cent of America's five and a half million farms have electricity. Im-

proved farm-to-market roads such as this one have done much to make rural life more pleasant and have aided farmers in more orderly and efficient marketing of their products. Of the U.S.A.'s three million miles of rural roads, about 60 per cent are surfaced.

Photo: USDA

253

Industrial Workers Talk Things Over

Concurrently with the effort to devise a satisfactory farm program there was a drive to improve the welfare of industrial workers. A shorter work day, higher wages, better working conditions, unemployment insurance, and collective bargaining were parts of the program spear-headed by the two largest labor unions, the American Federation of Labor and the Congress of Industrial Workers.

U.S. Department of Labor

Farm People Plan a Program

Out of the depression of the 1930's grew a farm program designed to regulate production to market demands; to maintain prices received by farmers for their products in line with prices paid by them for things they buy; to provide for more orderly marketing of farm products; and to conserve and build up the soil for the benefit of future generations. The farmer's "fair share of the consumer's dollar" was a primary goal. Aided by national, state, and county organizations, farmers and their families held endless meetings to debate the farm problem, suggest solutions, and devise means of carrying out the program voted into existence. Years of discussion of the farm problem in all its ramifications resulted in a greater realization on the part of rural people of the interrelationship of agriculture and the remainder of the economy and the significance of the fact that this country had become a creditor rather than a debtor nation. The American Farm Bureau Federation, the Farmer's Union, and the Grange have all contributed guidance.

Photo: USDA by Forsythe

The Supreme Court

The power of the United States resides in the people. Three independent and coequal branches of the government serve as checks on each other. The secret vote enables the people to change their elected officials, whenever that seems desirable, on election day. In 1788 a written Constitution was ratified as the law of the land and it established a Supreme Court to interpret the Constitution and head the judicial system, which includes many lower courts.

Photo: Architect of the Capitol

The President

A President elected for four years, and eligible for one additional four-year term, is chief of the executive branch.

Photo: Library of Congress

Congress

The legislative function is carried on by a Congress consisting of a Senate whose members serve for six years and a House of Representatives elected every two years. Each state has two senators. There is one representative for each district having approximately 350,000 population.

Photo: Architect of the Capitol

State Capitol of Iowa

Division of authority and responsibility among judicial, legislative, and executive branches is carried down through state, county, and city administrations. The forty-eight state governments closely resemble the federal pattern. A governor is chief executive, there is a legislature composed of a senate and house (except Nebraska, which has a unicameral legislature), and there is a supreme court with various lesser courts. State governments have various departments such as labor, agriculture, treasury, public roads, health, welfare, and others that function much as do their counterparts at the national level.

Photo: Library of Congress

County Courthouse, Romney, W. Va.

Each state is subdivided into counties, which carry out governmental functions in rural areas: law enforcement, road construction and maintenance, public schools, and welfare activities, all supported primarily by county-imposed taxes. The courthouse, usually located in the largest town in the county, is the center of government. Counties are partitioned into geographical units which are usually called townships.

Photo: Library of Congress

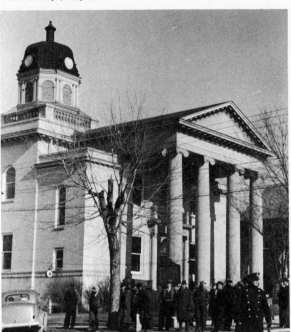

Town Hall, Connecticut

Cities, towns, and villages have their own municipal governments to carry out the many tasks created by congested areas. Most cities elect a mayor and council to run the city's affairs; some elect a commission whose members are responsible for a specific phase of work; other towns hire a nonpartisan manager trained in city administration. Law enforcement is an important function of city officials, since neither a county sheriff nor state police force have authority to act within the city and there are no federal police. The local policeman has become a popular figure. His primary function is to serve the people and protect their safety and property interests. Of course, they handle the occasional dangerous criminal with methods required by the situation.

Photo: Library of Congress

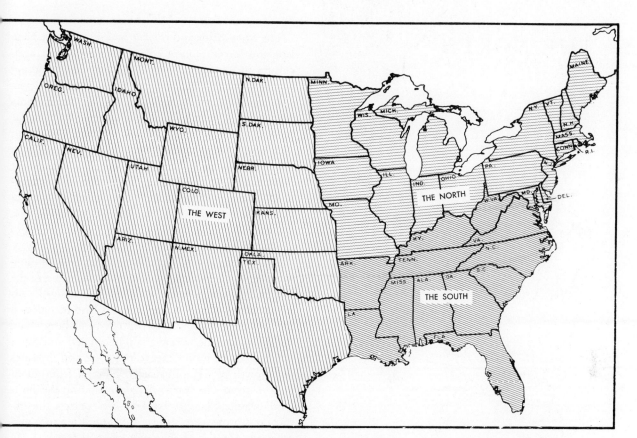

Map labels: WASH., OREG., CALIF., NEV., IDAHO, MONT., WYO., UTAH, COLO., ARIZ., N.MEX., N.DAK., S.DAK., NEBR., KANS., OKLA., TEX., MINN., WIS., MICH., IOWA, ILL., IND., OHIO, MO., ARK., TENN., KY., MISS., ALA., GA., LA., N.Y., VT., N.H., MASS., CONN., R.I., PA., W.VA., MD., DEL., VA., N.C., S.C., MAINE

THE WEST

THE NORTH

THE SOUTH

SOME POST WAR REGIONAL PATTERNS

To define the North, South, and West with precision is impossible, but, for general purposes, the South may be said to consist of states south of the Potomac and Ohio rivers and west from the Atlantic to include Arkansas and Louisiana. The West is made up of the Dakotas, Nebraska, Kansas, Oklahoma, and Texas and states west of them. The remaining nineteen states, containing only one fifth of the land area of the United States but half of the population, constitute the North.

THE NORTH

Cones of Industrial Expansion
A—1800   B—1840 TO 1900   C—1900 TO DATE

The stony fields and brief growing season in New England forced pioneer colonists to turn from agriculture to other means of livelihood. Shipbuilding, foreign trade, fishing, and merchandising soon developed as major enterprises. Most of the immigrants who began arriving in large numbers after 1820 at ports in Boston, New York, and Philadelphia spread west across the northern states, since few cared to go South and compete with slave labor. The concurrent rapid rise of the factory system gave these new immigrants the job opportunities they needed; industrial towns sprang up along the coast from Philadelphia north to Maine and west to Chicago, which began to grow rapidly after 1840. The delineation of three industrial triangles indicates the growth and development of the factory system and manufacturing in the North. The first of these triangles, indicating the situation about 1800, is a thin sliver of land included in the area comprising New York City, Pittsburgh, and Philadelphia. The second triangle is based on Boston and Baltimore, with Chicago the apex, and indicates the growth of the industrial revolution from about 1840 to 1900. The third triangle including the Portland, Maine, Chicago, Norfolk area reflects the tremendous growth in industrialization after 1900 and especially the rise of the automobile industry.

The Boston-Chicago-Baltimore triangle encompasses only about 4 per cent of the land area of the United States but 25 per cent of its population. Here are eight of our ten largest cities and in addition such industrial giants as Pittsburgh, Pennsylvania; Akron, Toledo, and Youngstown, Ohio; Gary, Indiana; Dearborn, Michigan; Schenectady, New York; and many others. The prodigious outpourings of thousands of factories, combined with the bountiful production of more than a half-million farms, makes this, in actual fact, a Golden Triangle. Within the Golden Triangle are immigrants or their descendants from practically every country on earth. Here is the melting pot where people of many races, cultures, and creeds rub shoulders every day and develop a sameness that is made more distinct by their differences.

The urban-rural pattern of the Golden Triangle remains essentially the same across the northern states with modifications imposed by regional variations. The Corn Belt is famed for agricultural production, but among its fields are factory towns turning out farm machinery and a wide range of manufactured products. The hustling, practical, skillful people of the North have not only created great wealth but a form of society that may be a pattern for other areas where many diverse cultures must exist side by side.

Pilgrims, Puritans, and Quakers from England and the Dutch, Swedes, Scots, and Germans who cast the mold and set the pattern of New England and the northern states in general had two outstanding characteristics—strong religious beliefs and great energy. Not to be a good church member was regrettable, but to be lazy and shiftless was unforgivable. A brisk climate accentuated the natural desire for energetic action, and scarcity of labor made it necessary for one to look after his own needs and to perform strenuous manual tasks. This necessity for personal toil made it appear a virtue, and those who preferred a more leisurely pace were labeled as unreliable and became virtual outcasts from respectable society.

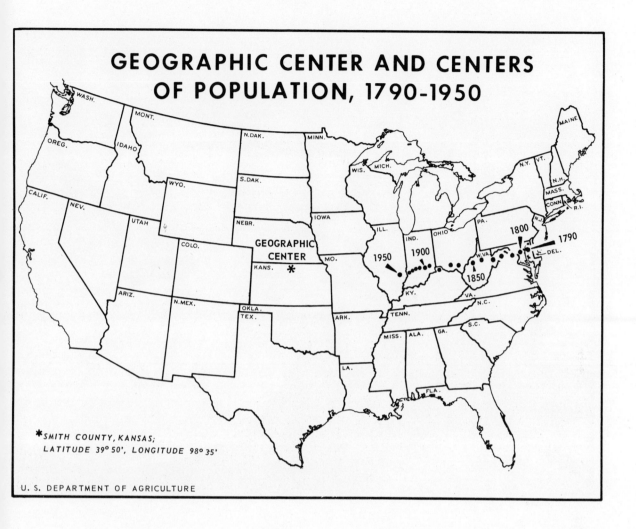

GEOGRAPHIC CENTER AND CENTERS OF POPULATION, 1790-1950

GEOGRAPHIC CENTER

1950 1900 1800 1790

1850

*SMITH COUNTY, KANSAS;
LATITUDE 39° 50', LONGITUDE 98° 35'

U. S. DEPARTMENT OF AGRICULTURE

Centers of Population

In 1790 the center of population was twenty-three miles east of Baltimore, Maryland. Ten years later it had shifted west of Baltimore eighteen miles, and continued a steady march west, as the frontier receded inland, at a rate of about fifty miles per decade. The distance between the stars indicates the amount of growth during the ten-year period between censuses. The geographical center is in Kansas some four hundred and fifty miles west of the 1950 center of population.

Map: U.S.D.A.

New Amsterdam Became a City of Eight Million People

The largest population center of the North and of the nation is New York City. Manhattan Island, site of the small thrifty Dutch town of New Amsterdam in 1650, is now crowded with two million people representing practically every nation on earth. This aerial photograph taken from a height of 26,000 feet shows Manhattan Island in the center surrounded by its sprawling thickly populated environs. At the left of Manhattan Island is Henry Hudson's river leading off to the north and on the right the East River meandering out to Long Island Sound. To the left of the great harbor and barely discernible stands the Statue of Liberty, on Bedloe Island, holding aloft the torch in which the flame of liberty never dies.

Photo: U.S. Air Force

Fort Pitt Grew into Pittsburgh

The industrial heart of this nation is Pittsburgh, on the Forks of the Ohio, where much blood was spilt in the bitter struggle to control the Old Northwest Territory in the days of French and British wars in which Indians and colonists had a part. Here, in the arsenal of democracy, coal and iron ore are converted into steel, which in turn becomes tanks, guns, ships, airplanes, bridges, skyscrapers, and baby buggies. The Monongahela and Allegheny rivers, which converged form the Ohio River, played a major role in transporting immigrants to the West in early days and now carry a heavier tonnage of coal, ore, steel, and other industrial products than any other rivers in America.

Photo: Pennsylvania State Department of Commerce

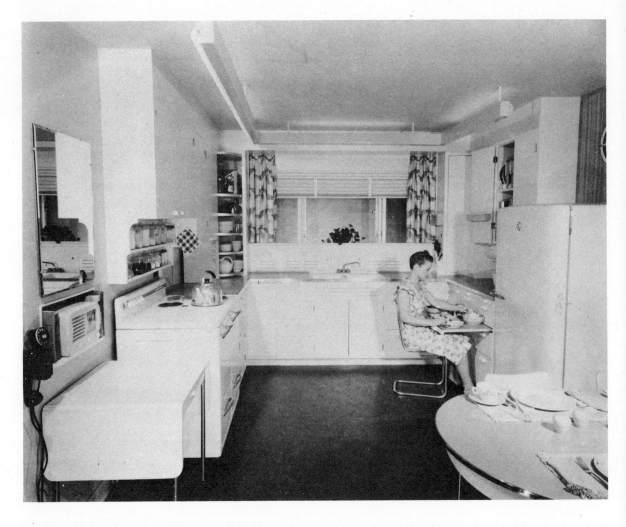

Industry Creates House Appliances

Among the many useful and labor-saving devices produced in the shops and factories of the North, those designed to make housework simpler and easier hold an important place. Shown here is a modern kitchen with an electric refrigerator, deep freeze, dishwasher, range, ironer, radio, telephone, revolving shelves, indirect lighting, electric fan, and other equipment arranged to reduce walking, stooping, and stretching. Not all families can afford such a kitchen, but efficient production and marketing, combined with easy credit facilities and a high level of income for ordinary workers, have made it possible for most homes to have many modern conveniences. A visitor from abroad has said that the most surprising thing about this country is that American homes actually look like the pictures carried in the magazines he had seen at home.

Photo: USDA by Meade

The Little Red School House Has Come and Gone

Small country school districts have been consolidated and large, centrally located, well-equipped schools constructed to which children are brought by bus. In towns and cities, modern schools have been built to provide for the thirty-five million children from ages six to sixteen who are required by law to attend school. During the first twelve years of their education, about 85 per cent of the children attend public schools. Approximately half of the students complete the twelfth grade and nearly half of them continue on to a college or university. Over two and a half million students are enrolled in colleges and universities in the United States, of whom more than thirty thousand are from foreign countries. Adults continue their education especially in night schools and through correspondence courses and other programs in which approximately fifty million participate annually.

A Parent-Teacher Association is organized in most public schools and in many private ones to maintain a close working relationship between parents and teachers in improving programs of study and other school activities.

Photo: Division of Visual Education

Spilt Milk

This remarkable picture of a splash of milk drama-
tizes the importance of milk in the economy of the
Great Lakes and Northeast states. The interaction of
soil, precipitation, temperatures, length of growing
season, lay of the land, temperament and characteristics of people, labor supply, proximity to market,
and other factors determine the geography of agriculture. The Northeastern and Great Lakes states
contain many millions of people so that there is a
ready market for fluid milk and for butter, cheese,
and ice cream. That this is our principal dairy region,
however, is also a result of cold climate, rough, tim-
bered terrain, and the northern European dairyland
ancestry of a large part of the farm population of this
area. It requires a calm, steady, highly civilized person to match the twice-a-day regularity of a placid
milk cow. The preponderance of cheese and butter
production in Wisconsin, Minnesota, and Michigan
as compared to the Eastern dairy region reflects the
relatively thin market there for direct consumption of
fluid milk.

Photo: Charles T. Bradford Co., Edgerton

Temptation

Corn and hogs have become synonymous with the Middle West. The Corn Belt developed in answer to a persistent demand for pork and favorable soil and climatic conditions, coupled with the establishment of family-size farms headed by energetic, independent-minded men of the dirt-farmer type who loved the soil and liked to do their own work. The hog pictured here is confronted with a difficult decision. The wires separating the hog from the coveted ear of corn are charged with electricity. The hog knows that if it touches a wire it will get a shock, not enough to hurt but uncomfortable and nerve-tingling. On the other hand, that ear of corn would be good eating. So——

Photo: Rural Electrification Administration

The Judas Goat Leads the Way

The Middle West is dotted with stockyards and meat-packing plants, but Chicago continues to have the greatest of all. Out in front of an unsuspecting flock of sheep in the Chicago stockyards strides the sly and cunning "Judas Goat," who entices the sheep to follow him to the slaughterhouse. There the treacherous leader sidles quickly out a side gate while the sheep go on to destruction. The Judas Goat, whose horns have been removed to aid in deceiving the poor "lambs," hurries back to lead another group of sheep down the way of no return.

Photo: Abernethy Livestock Photo Company

Quarrying Marble in Vermont

The staunch and rugged character of New Englanders has been likened to the green hills of Vermont underlaid with marble. In any event, marble quarrying is a major industry in Vermont. Here blocks are being cut for large interior entrance columns and pilasters of the White House during its 1953 restoration.

Photo: Vermont Marble Co., Proctor, Vt.

Automobiles Parked Outside a Plant

The industrial activity of the North is greatly diversified, but the most spectacular is undoubtedly the automobile industry. Since 1900, more than a hundred and thirty-six million cars, trucks, and buses have been made in the United States, many of them in the North. Shown here is a portion of the 113 acres of parking lots required for the use of the 63,000 men and women employed at the River Rouge plant of the Ford Motor Company at Dearborn, Michigan. Workers in automobile factories have an average annual income of more than five thousand dollars.

Photo: Ford Motor Company

Superhighways to Handle Traffic

A clamor for good roads persisted from colonial days, but it was not until the coming of the automobile that sufficient pressure developed to get federal and state governments to provide hard-surfaced roads throughout the nation. With over fifty-six million motor vehicles traveling five hundred and fifty billion miles per year along three and a third million miles of highway at an average of seventeen vehicles per mile, carefully designed and regulated roads be-

came essential. Traffic fatalities average about thirty-eight thousand annually or approximately seven per hundred million vehicle miles. One of the first superhighways was the Pennsylvania Turnpike, pictured above, connecting Philadelphia and Pittsburgh, which has no cross traffic and which by-passes towns and cities. It will be recalled that one of the first East-West roads built in colonial days was one connecting the seaport, Philadelphia, with Pittsburgh on the Ohio River.

Photo: Pennsylvania Turnpike Commission

Railroads Leading into Washington, D.C.

New York City was the first capital of the United States, but later the seat of government was shifted to Philadelphia, where it remained for ten years. Meanwhile, after a compromise between North and South, a ten-mile-square area named in honor of Christopher Columbus was laid out on the Potomac River as a future federal city. The Frenchman L'Enfant drew magnificent plans, the basic features of which have finally been achieved. In 1800, President and Mrs. John Adams moved into the unfinished Executive Mansion, which since 1814 has been called the White House. The same year Congress moved into the north wing of the Capitol Building, but the cast-iron dome was not put into place until 1863. The Washington Monument was started in 1848, but work proceeded slowly and was halted entirely for more than 20 years and was finally completed in 1884. Growth of population reflects the increasing importance of Washington in national and international affairs. In 1800, the population of the new little capital city totaled only 14,000; following the Civil War (1870) it had risen to 132,000; at the end of World War II (1950) it was 802,000. This picture of Union Station seems to indicate that all railroads lead to Washington.

Photo: Association of American Railroads

A Half Century of Aviation Growth

World War II gave tremendous impetus to air travel, and every year since has brought new developments, with old records displaced by new ones, which in turn are quickly shattered. There are more than five thousand airports in the United States. This one in Kansas City, Missouri, serves more than twenty-five million passengers and handles millions of tons of freight and mail.

Photo: Chamber of Commerce, Kansas City, Mo.

Moth-Ball Fleet in the Hudson

During the period 1940–45 the U.S. government built 1,881 freight ships, of which 1,798 were dismantled, treated with preservatives, and put in inactive reserve after the war. Shown here is a part of the "moth-ball fleet" being held in the Hudson River for possible future use. Some of the idle ships have been used for storing grain for later shipment abroad, when normal storage facilities have been overcrowded. During World War II American shipping companies built over six hundred freighters, all of which were kept in service for peacetime use.

U.S. Naval Photographic Service

Freighters on the Great Lakes

The five Great Lakes, named from east to west Ontario, Erie, Huron, Michigan, and Superior, have been significant in the history of the Middle West from earliest times. Upon their shores are some of the largest and commercially most important cities in the United States. Buffalo, New York, lying at the eastern end of Lake Erie, was the western terminus of the Erie Canal and is connected with the Atlantic Ocean by Lake Ontario and the St. Lawrence River that flows into the sea. Cleveland and Toledo, Ohio; Detroit, Michigan; Chicago, Illinois; and Milwaukee, Wisconsin, have benefited by their location on the Great Lakes. From Duluth and Superior, Minnesota, at the western tip of Lake Superior, iron ore is shipped east to be converted into steel. In order to get through the locks of the Sault Sainte Marie Canal, nicknamed the "Soo," connecting Lakes Huron and Superior, freighters are long and narrow with many individual compartments. Ships like those pictured carry loads of over ten thousand tons of grain or ore.

Photo: Michigan Tourist Council

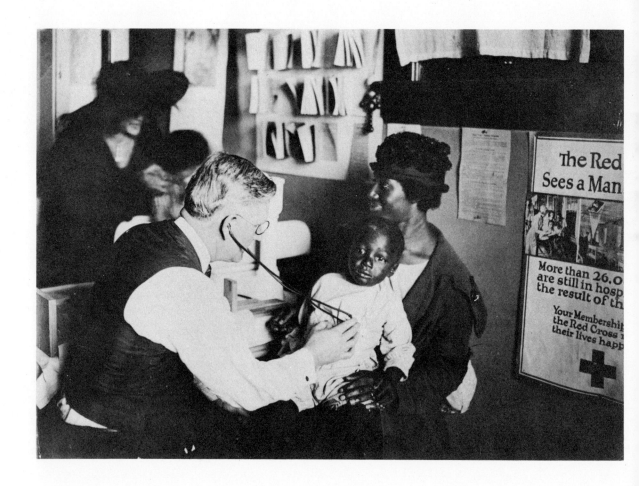

A Doctor Examines a Patient

Not long ago a foreigner, newly arrived in New York City, was taken ill. Doctors were mystified about his sickness until he broke out with smallpox; none of the doctors had ever treated a case of this disease and they failed to recognize symptoms. Only a few decades ago, smallpox, yellow fever, and many other plagues which have now been brought under control ravaged the population, leaving death, heartbreak, and terror in their wake. The real unsung heroes of the long past are the courageous medical scientists of all lands who have risked their lives that others might live. In the United States, the list has many distinguished names, including Dr. W. T. G. Morton of Massachusetts, who popularized the use of anesthetics, which were probably first used by Dr. Crawford Long of Georgia; and Dr. Walter Reed, who solved the problem of yellow fever.

Within the last century, tremendous progress has been made in the prevention of disease and its treatment, and in hospital techniques, surgical skills, and easing of pain. Accumulated knowledge and its wide and quick dissemination have contributed to the gains made. Perhaps equally important, however, has been the banishment of fear and superstition with a corollary increase in willingness to accept and utilize new techniques and medication. Also important has been general acknowledgment that any disease outbreak anywhere is a menace to all. The Public Health Service of the U.S. Department of Health, Education and Welfare is a far-flung organization devoted to the conquest of disease and improvement of health, with emphasis on research, medical and hospital services, and public health practices. In the United States, there is a physician for each eight hundred people, a dentist for each two thousand people, a hospital bed for each ten people, and generally a hospital within twenty miles of any point.

Photo: National Archives

Flowers and Birds in Pennsylvania

Indications of the maturing of the United States and its growing appreciation of aesthetic values are such manifestations as this lamppost decorated with a flower urn and charming birdhouse in the streets of Somerset, Pennsylvania.

Photo: by Bowen, Somerset, Pa., Chamber of Commerce

South Stafford, Vermont

New England villages and towns retain their charm and beauty despite heavy industrialization and the influx of many people of varied ancestral backgrounds not closely related to the Puritan tradition.

Photo: USDA by Knoblock

Where the South Begins

With an annual rainfall of four to five feet, the South is a land of many rivers and streams which have been, and are now, among its greatest assets. These lazy rivers and languid streams provided easy highways for pioneer settlers pushing inland and later for transporting crops to markets and for intercourse between upcountry communities and seacoast ports.

Here, the Mississippi River, meandering down from the north, is joined by the Ohio River sweeping in from the northeast. As one mighty river, they roll through the South a thousand miles to New Orleans and the Gulf of Mexico.

When northern rivers, swollen by melting snows, empty into southern streams running bankful from prolonged spring rains, gigantic floods result, which cause great losses of life and property. High levees, restraining dams, emergency reservoirs, reforestation, and other man-made devices have been employed to alleviate such disastrous floods, but they still occur occasionally, just as they did in 1541 when the intrepid Spanish explorer, Hernando de Soto, witnessed a tremendous flood along the Mississippi River. According to one narrative, "The flood was forty days in reaching its greatest height which was the twentieth of April, and it was a beautiful thing to look upon the sea where there had been fields, for on each side of the river the water extended over twenty leagues of land, and all of this area was navigated by canoes, and nothing was seen but the tops of the tallest trees."

Photo: Cairo, Ill., Association of Commerce

THE SOUTH

South of the Ohio and Potomac rivers and westward from the Atlantic Ocean to the bayous of Louisiana and the cotton fields of Arkansas lies a land that no one really knows. It is a land of extremes. Over the years, novelists, movie makers, and some historians have emphasized the extremes and, through repetition, these extremes have become accepted as typical. For example, the impression seems to be that people are not "just people" in the South. Either they are gentle folk of sugary sweetness and nobility of character, dressed in the finest of clothes and living in mansions with white columns, or they are riffraff dwelling in rural slums. The Negro population has been represented as being either the lovable, subservient "Mammy" or "Uncle Remus" type endowed with the wisdom of the ages or crap-shooting, razor-toting, trifling, no-account rapscallions. The fact is that the majority of southerners are hard-working, conscientious, churchgoing people intent on trying to create a better life for themselves and their communities. In this, the South differs very little from other sections of our country. But the South has inherited from the past difficult social, economic, and political problems.

The concept of the ante-bellum South as having only a two-layer society with nothing in the middle but "white trash" is not in accordance with facts. In 1850, in the twelve principal cotton states, there were only 74,000 plantations, that is, places using only slave labor, out of a total of 569,000 farms and plantations. In Montgomery County, Alabama, in the heart of the Cotton South, three out of four farmers were land-owners having up to two hundred acres. The evidence seems conclusive that planters and farmers in the ante-bellum South were divided among large, medium, and small operators. The wealthy planter group represented a classical example of conspicuous consumption, and they so dominated the limelight that only careful research based on property records has revealed that in the years prior to the Civil War, as now, there was a large but unpretentious group of substantial farmers. During the Civil War, it is probable that relatively few of these farmers waved a sword and ordered a charge, but they fought as gallantly as any soldiers ever did.

The South as defined here includes twelve states having a land area of about three hundred and forty-two million acres of which some 60 per cent is in farms. To those steeped in the idea of the South as one huge cotton field, it is surprising to learn that nearly six out of every ten acres in the South is forest land, that lumbering is a major business, and, because of relatively rapid tree growth, the South will be our principal source of lumber in the future. Significant, too, is the fact that forest operations in the South are relatively a "small-fellow" enterprise with the average size of forest—ninety-six acres—being exactly the same size as the average Southern farm.

It is disappointing to some visitors to find that the Southern rural landscape generally does not have the "curried and combed" appearance of some Northern farm communities. Sometimes this somewhat disheveled appearance is attributed to laziness and related sins; however, the fact is the South will not entirely eliminate this situation so long as it continues to be predominantly a tobacco, cotton, and forest area. The reason is that cotton and tobacco are both intensive crops; that is, acreages are small and usually are shifted year by year from one cleared spot to another on the farm. A comparison between corn and tobacco acreages will illustrate the point. The average acreage of corn in the United States is nearly eight times that of tobacco, which means that in corn country a much larger percentage of the land is neatly plowed and cared for compared to that in tobaccoland. In the Deep South most cotton is grown in small patches rather than in extensive fields. The same situation prevails in respect to most Southern crops, including corn, of which the South has twenty million acres. A generous painting of farm buildings across the South would enhance its appearance, but anyone who knew the South of the 1920's and that of today cannot help but marvel at the progress and improvement that has been made. The shift from crops to livestock with a consequent clearing of scrub-tree land and improved pastures has done a face-lifting job in many areas. Enhanced farm incomes and an expanded industry providing full and part-time employment to many people have helped raise the standard of living.

Everywhere in the South can be seen the plants and factories resulting from the tremendous industrial development that has been going on at an accelerated pace in recent decades. The fact that three fourths of the cotton spindles are now below the Mason-Dixon Line, whereas the reverse was true at the turn of the century, is perhaps the most striking evidence of the dynamic New South.

In the Land of Cotton

Recovery of the Southern economy was long delayed and made more difficult by the depletion of soils resulting from generations of one-crop farming. Raising tobacco or cotton year after year without adequate replacement of plant nutrients caused general deterioration of the standard of living. The sharecropper system encouraged exploitation of the soil and a general disregard for care of houses, buildings, fences, and equipment because many croppers moved to a different farm each year. The increased ownership of farms by both Negro and white croppers has aided in stabilizing the farm population with consequent better care of farmhouses and other property. Cropper-operated farms now comprise only about 2 per cent of the U.S. land in farms, cropland, and value of farm products sold.

Photo: Library of Congress

A Farm in the Piedmont

The turn of the century meant also the turn of the South from the painful road of recovery onto the high road of an expanding and healthier economy. Industrialization, which had been growing slowly but steadily for two decades, began to spread rapidly, especially as the development of hydroelectric power became important. The shift from cotton to tobacco, peanuts, fruit, vegetables, rice, cattle, and the like, improved road and railroad transportation, better farming practices, expanded credit facilities, an increasing industrial activity, the conquest of malaria, pellagra, etc., and a flourishing tourist trade all combined to energize the South's economy.

A brief review of the Tennessee Valley Authority project will serve to indicate the sort of activity which has taken place throughout the South in recent years.

Photo: USDA by Blake

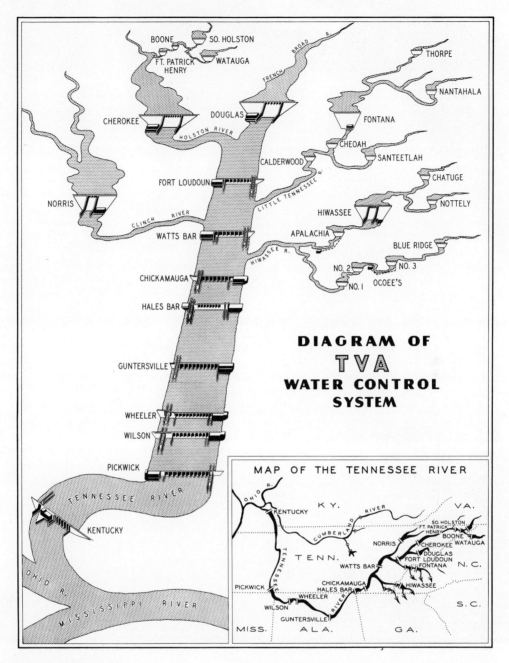

DIAGRAM OF
TVA
WATER CONTROL
SYSTEM

MAP OF THE TENNESSEE RIVER

Tennessee Valley Authority

In 1933 the T.V.A. was empowered by Congress to undertake a gigantic project designed to reduce flood damage, generate electric power, and provide navigation up the Tennessee River to Knoxville. The area normally has a rainfall of forty to sixty inches, so that irrigation does not enter into consideration and the T.V.A. is not an irrigation project. Along the Tennessee River at irregular intervals of approximately fifty to sixty miles are nine dams designed to provide flood control, navigation, and electric power. In addi-

tion there are nineteen such multiple-purpose dams on upstream tributaries of the Tennessee. Others are being constructed at strategically located points on the main branches arising in the Blue Ridge Mountains and Great Smokies. From Knoxville in the eastern mountains to Paducah, Kentucky, where the Tennessee River empties into the Ohio, is a distance of six hundred and fifty miles in which the river drops eight hundred and fifteen feet or about 1¼ feet per mile.

Photo: T.V.A.

Flood Control

By holding back water runoff from hundreds of mountain streams and regulating the flow downriver, dams greatly reduced damage from the twenty-one floods which occurred during the fifteen-year period, 1936–51. Norris Dam on the Clinch River in east Tennessee is typical of the dams on tributary rivers and streams. Norris has a storage reservoir with a capacity of two and one-half million acre-feet of water. It also has a power installation of two 50,000 kilowatt units.

Photo: T.V.A.

Navigation

The series of dams along the Tennessee River has created a depth of at least nine feet, which enables large river craft to haul coal, grain, oil, and other supplies and merchandise the entire 650 miles up the river to Knoxville, winter or summer. Here the *Delta Queen* goes through locks at Kentucky Dam.

Photo: T.V.A.

Multiple Purpose Dam

This is a view looking upstream at Fort Loudoun Dam, the farthest up the Tennessee River. Fort Loudoun is 122 feet high, 4,190 feet long, and its lake covers 14,500 acres. It is a multiple-purpose dam, combining the generation of electricity with flood control and navigation. Its giant locks (at the right) must be opened upon request to allow even a rowboat to pass through.

Photo: T.V.A.

Electric Power Turbines

The T.V.A. has a total installed capacity of 3,400,-000 kilowatts provided by twenty-nine hydroelectric-power dams, six steam plants, and a number of minor hydro and steam plants. Demand for electrical current has increased sharply in recent years for farm, factory, town, and city, and to meet these needs a number of large steam plants have been constructed to double the generating capacity of T.V.A. It is anticipated that within a few years these steam plants will be using ten million tons of coal per year, most of which will be hauled on the Tennessee River from Kentucky coal fields.

In general, electrical power generated by the T.V.A. is disposed of on a wholesale basis to public and private agencies which do the retailing. In a recent year, a little more than half of the electric energy went to municipalities and cooperatives, 16 per cent was used by federal agencies, primarily for defense purposes, 26 per cent went directly to industries, and 7 per cent to other power systems.

Photo: T.V.A.

Fertilizer, Grass, and Trees

The years of urging conservation practices resulted in widespread use of methods to conserve soil and water resources. A few years ago these two fields in Madison County, North Carolina, were equally gullied. The owner of the field at the left, through the use of phosphate and lime, produced cover that halts erosion and provides grazing for livestock. The T.V.A. has carried on test demonstrations on thousands of farms in the valley in which the results of better seed, fertilizer, and farm practices can readily be seen.

Photo: T.V.A.

Recreation

Lakes created by the dams have been stocked with fish and sportsmen find them favorite haunts. Boating, swimming, and other water sports attract thousands of visitors annually.

Photo: T.V.A.

A College That Tobacco Built

James B. Duke perfected a cigarette-making machine and made millions of dollars in the tobacco business. Contributions from Mr. Duke and his family made possible the transformation of small Trinity College of Durham, North Carolina, into magnificent Duke University, of which the main part of the campus can be seen here. J. B. Duke had this advice for young people: "Walk while you are young so that you can ride when you are old." Tobacco, the South's first cash crop and the commercial mainstay of the colonists at Jamestown, continues to be of great importance. In a recent year, United States farmers produced 2,255,000,000 pounds of tobacco, which they sold for an average price of fifty cents a pound. Approximately 80 per cent of the production is used for cigarettes, 8 per cent for cigars, and 11 per cent for smoking and chewing tobacco and snuff.

Photo: North Carolina State Department Conservation and Development

Mechanical Cotton Picker

One of the most outstanding and far-reaching developments in the South has been the fulfillment of the long-time dream, a mechanical cotton picker. The machines cost several thousand dollars so that only a relatively few planters operating large cotton acreages can afford them; however, smaller farmers sometimes join together in buying a cotton picker as they have in buying combines and other types of heavy farm machinery. Mechanization has furthered education; expensive equipment cannot be turned over to illiterate, irresponsible, untrained people. Machines such as the one pictured have aided in overcoming labor shortages and enabled the planter to bring his crop to market at an earlier date. Such machines require about two man-hours per acre compared to fifty man-hours for hand picking.

Photo: U.S. Extension Service

Brahman Cattle Aid the South

Most breeds of cattle in this country originated in Great Britain and northern Europe. They do not perspire freely through the skin and suffer during long hot summers in the South.

Brahman cattle from India are unique in that they have more skin surface than ordinary cattle and also have sweat glands which enable them to withstand hot weather much better than other cattle. Crossbreeding of Brahman cattle with domestic breeds, such as Herefords, has gone on for years to develop a beeftype animal that could thrive under hot weather conditions. The first successful crossing of cattle from India and a domestic breed occurred in Texas when Brahman bulls were used on Shorthorn cows and a new breed called Santa Gertrudis was developed.

With mild winters permitting year-round grazing and new breeds suitable to the area, the South is rapidly becoming a major beef-producing area.

The name Brahman for the India cattle is said to have been acquired through a misunderstanding when the first shipment arrived at quarantine in New York. The attendants were of the high caste known as Brahman and were wearing turbans. When someone asked them what they (the cattle) were, the men from India, thinking the question had been inspired by the turbans, proudly replied "Brahman."

Photo: by Chesnut, Alabama Polytechnic Institute

The New South

This beautiful, modern home was built after World War II on a 3,500-acre Alabama farm on which all the land is in grass to produce beef cattle.

Photo: S.C.S.

Birthplace of Memorial Day

May 30 has been set aside as Memorial Day, when it is customary to decorate the graves of loved ones who have passed on, especially those who have died in the service of their country. This thoughtful service got its start in 1866 when three women of Columbus, Mississippi, decorated the graves of Confederate soldiers and graciously laid flowers on the graves of Federal soldiers buried in the cemetery. When Judge Francis M. Finch of Ithaca, New York, read a newspaper account of the friendly incident, he wrote a poem, "The Blue and the Gray," to commemorate the three women—Miss Matt Morton, Mrs. J. T. Fontaine, and Mrs. G. T. Hill. General John A. Logan, encouraged by his wife, issued an official order as Chief of Staff making Memorial Day an annual event, and the custom has become general throughout the country. This scene shows a monument to the Confederate soldier in the Columbus cemetery surrounded by modern-day girls carrying flowers and Confederate flags. At the extreme right is Mrs. J. I. Sturdivant, a niece of Miss Matt Morton.

Photo: Columbus, Miss., Chamber of Commerce

Country Church

A visitor from abroad expressed surprise that in the American college town in which he was a student there were more churches than motion-picture houses. Actually, that is true throughout the United States: there are only some eighteen thousand motion-picture theaters as compared to about three hundred thousand church buildings. In fact, the number of churches exceeds by more than seven to one the total number of all places of amusement including, in addition to movie theaters and numerous other familiar centers of recreation, such places as billiard and pool halls, bowling alleys, dance halls, race tracks, swimming pools, and skating rinks.

Many country churches have consolidated with neighboring congregations in order to constitute a stronger and more effective group, but others, such as this one, maintain a loyal following. The horse and buggy has disappeared and has been replaced by the automobile; however, some farmers use the pickup truck as shown here for driving to church as well as for other purposes. The United States is a churchgoing land.

Photo: Courtesy of Frank Parker

A Soldier Samples Fruit

An important factor in the economic welfare of the South is the maintenance of many military establishments for training Army, Navy, Marine Corps, and Air Force officers and troops. Here a G.I. good-naturedly samples fruit from the wide variety of fruit and melons at a roadside stand near Spartanburg, South Carolina. The typical American soldier, like the nation itself, is willing to do whatever has to be done to maintain peace, but he is always ready and anxious to relax, have fun, and proceed on a friendly basis.

Photo: USDA by Osborne

King of the Mules

Americans love festivals, and every little industry must have a festival all its own, with its Grand Champion, Beauty Queen, and Governor in solicitous attendance. Here "Brown Sunshire," Grand Champion Mule at the Columbia, Tennessee, Mule Day Festival, proudly wears his crown and poses with the Festival Queen and Governor of Tennessee.

Photo: Chamber of Commerce, Columbia, Tenn.

The Iron Man at Birmingham, Alabama

Birmingham, Alabama, an industrial city, is sometimes called the Pittsburgh of the South. However, during the War Between the States when manufacturing plants were the South's greatest need, there was not even a village where Birmingham now stands. Founded in 1871, where two railroad lines crossed, Birmingham benefited by being planned and laid out prior to settlement. The metropolitan area has a population of over a half million, most of them related to the manufacture of more than thirty-two hundred commercial products. Coal, iron ore, and limestone are basic materials necessary in the manufacture of iron and steel. In the vicinity of Birmingham, they are found within twenty miles of each other. No other city or area in the United States and perhaps in the world has such a favorable combination of essential materials so close at hand.

Photo: by McAlexander, Birmingham, Ala., Chamber of Commerce

A Negro Farm Home in Mississippi

Every profession has its competent Negroes and the number increases every year. There is a trend toward home improvement by colored families, including farmers, who now live in modern homes such as the one shown here, although many live in much more ordinary homes on plantations and small farms. Mr. and Mrs. Isaac Daniels, cotton and rice farmers of Mound Bayou, Mississippi, are inspecting a beautiful hibiscus plant.

Photo: USDA by Briscoe

Miami Beach, Florida

Many warm, sunny days in the Deep South during winter and cool refreshing ocean breezes during summer months have made beaches along the lower Atlantic and the Gulf Coast popular havens, both winter and summer, for many generations. By attracting tourists and vacationers from all parts of the country and providing a pleasant retreat in a mild climate, beaches and resorts are an important source of income. One of the most famous of the vacation spots is Miami Beach, Florida, a section of which is shown here.

Photo: Florida State News Bureau

Gone with the Wind

In 1939, Selznick International produced the Technicolor motion picture, *Gone with the Wind*, based on the book by Margaret Mitchell. Vivien Leigh, Clark Gable, and a brilliant supporting cast made the picture perhaps the most famous of all times. This romantic and exciting story of the Civil War period dramatized the disappearance of a world which had its charm but one which few, if any, Southerners would want again. The New South has much of the good and little of the bad that characterized the Old South of nostalgic memory.

It took a Northerner like Stephen Foster to express in sentimental song the feeling that Americans everywhere have for the South, with its cotton and magnolias, its share croppers and tobacco farmers, its warm sunny days and balmy evenings, its showboats and the *Robert E. Lee,* its courteous, soft-spoken people, regardless of color, its piney woods and fine fishing, its mountain resorts and seaside beaches, its fantastic past and its bright future.

Photo: Courtesy Loew's Inc. and Selznick International

THE WEST

Ever since a little group of courageous people headed west from the comparative security and comfort of the Bay Colony in Massachusetts for the Connecticut Valley more than three hundred years ago, there has been no more fascinating phrase to the American people than the "West."

Over the years the "West" has meant many things to many people. To explorers who first traversed the West, its wonders were viewed primarily from the standpoint of a sightseer. To fur traders who followed, it meant opportunities for trade and a chance to get rich by exchanging a few cheap manufactured articles for the fabulous furs of the Indians. The hunters and trappers who were next to go into the wilderness were attracted less by the chance for profits to be quickly squandered than by the life of splendid isolation in a hunter's paradise swarming with deer, bear, mountain lions, beaver, antelope, elk, and buffalo. To the rough, tough miners grubbing for gold and blinded to all else, the West meant only a place where one might "strike it rich." By reducing wild life, especially the vast herds of buffalo, hunters cleared the way for the cattlemen with their large herds roaming the open range. These Cattle Kings reveled in the rough but picturesque life on the plains with "wild and woolly" cowboys riding herd on far-flung possessions. Finally came the farmer with his plow. To him the West meant an opportunity to subdue its wildness and to bring its fertile and watered areas under cultivation. To others the West meant escape from "the law," monotony, debts, religious intolerance, tragedy at home, or unrequited love.

Thus on the frontier could be found all sorts and conditions of men (and a few women), all stirred by some inner restlessness and determination which compelled those who survived to undergo hardships, dangers, and loneliness under grueling conditions.

The weak perished or turned back; the "winning of the West" was accomplished by the adventurous, stouthearted, and physically rugged.

Life on the ever-shifting frontier was unlike anything its inhabitants had previously experienced, and many adjustments and adaptations were necessitated. There are those who hold that characteristics of the American people generally thought of as typical stemmed from repeated contact with frontier conditions by overlapping waves of the westward movement. For example, it is claimed that the continual shifting about of the American people (in 1952, nine out of every ten persons had moved at least once in his lifetime) is a result of generation after generation acting on Horace Greeley's advice to "go West and grow up with the country." Many an American can say in all truth that no two of his forebears are buried in the same state. The careless wastefulness of Americans has also been attributed, in large part, to the presence during a long period of a frontier where one could find new, rich land to replace old soil worn out by exploitation. A free and easy manner and a disregard for conventions considered so important in an older society resulted, it is claimed, from frontier conditions where everybody was a stranger, time was short, and a person was accepted on the basis of current performance rather than on a past record, family name, or size of bank roll. An optimistic habit of thought has also been laid to the fact that throughout our history, if conditions became unsatisfactory in a certain place, one could always move on to "greener pastures" in the West.

A preference for a democratic form of government was undoubtedly strengthened by the experience of those who set up countless local governmental units among strongly individualistic people where no other form of rule would have been long tolerated.

Bronco-Busting Remains
a Popular Western Sport

The Old West lives on in rodeos, "dude ranches," movies, ballads, songs, and stories, and in the wearing of cowboy hats, boots, and related paraphernalia. In many Western communities, a rodeo is an annual event at which cowboys compete in roping contests, bronco-busting (riding wild, bucking horses), bull-dogging steers (leaping from a galloping horse onto a frantically running steer and throwing the animal to the ground by its horns), and many other stirring and dangerous events. The "Pendleton Roundup" in Oregon, the "Frontier Day" celebration at Cheyenne, Wyoming, and many other annual rodeo and pioneer-day celebrations attract thousands of visitors from all parts of the country.

Photo: Cheyenne, Wyo., Frontier Day

The Dude Ranch Provides Fun for Vacationers

In the last twenty-five years, the dude ranch has become a popular vacation spot where the tenderfoot visitor can wear cowboy clothes, ride horseback over romantic trails through enchanting scenery, and for a brief while feel that he is a part of the romantic and exciting West of long ago.

Photo: Union Pacific Railroad

Will Rogers Typified the West

Will Rogers, who said that he never had met a man he didn't like, typified the openhanded, good-natured, easygoing, carelessly dressed Westerner. Raised on an Oklahoma cattle ranch, Rogers, who was part Indian, performed a trick roping act in vaudeville to which he added humorous remarks that made him famous throughout the world. A strong advocate of airplanes during their infancy, he was killed in a plane accident in Alaska while on a world tour in 1935.

Photo: Architect of the Capitol

WHR Helmsman III

Range cattle of the longhorn type could not compete with improved breeds and gradually purebred herds have been developed throughout the West. One of the outstanding purebred establishments is the Wyoming Hereford Ranch, which has had three bulls each of whose progeny sold for over a million dollars. The ranch was offered $100,000 for one of these bulls, named WHR Helmsman III (shown above), but the owner turned down the offer, saying that he wouldn't know what to do with the $100,000, but he did know what to do with the bull. The founder of the ranch gave up a career as a business executive and developed the ranch in an effort to regain his health. Out of gratitude for living some twenty years longer than the doctors had predicted, he left the 60,000-acre ranch to be operated as a nonprofit organization, with all income to go into Christian missionary work throughout the world.

Photo: by Glover, Kansas City, Mo.

A Wild Stallion in Wyoming

The bands of wild horses that roamed the Old West are also disappearing. In the old days, cowboys would chase a herd trying desperately to lasso an animal that appealed to them. It was noted that when first alarmed the horse pack would run in a straight line for ten or twelve miles, then circle back to their old grazing ground. Acting upon this knowledge, cowboys on fresh mounts would be placed along the back trail to keep the wild mustangs running until they became exhausted and easily corralled. In recent years airplanes have been used to round up wild bunches and skillfully drive them into a dead-end canyon or carefully constructed trap where men on horseback keep them controlled until they have been subdued. Horses bearing brands are returned to their owners upon payment of a roundup fee; of the remainder, the better specimens are broken for saddle horses, the bucking broncos are sold for use at rodeos, and the "culls" are disposed of to packers for two or three cents per pound to be made into dog food.

Perhaps the most famous, as well as most beautiful, of all wild horses was the handsome Palomino stallion pictured above at the time of his capture in the Red Desert of Wyoming in 1945 and given the name "Desert Dust." Although the ancestry of this horse is uncertain, he may have been a descendant of a Kentucky stallion which escaped to the wilds of Wyoming with two mares in 1903 and was never recaptured. The five-year-old, cream-colored, silver-maned Desert Dust weighed 1,200 pounds and was the leader of a band of thirty mares and colts when captured.

Geyser in Yellowstone Park

The natural beauty of the West's most famous peaks, waterfalls, caverns, historic sites, and rare works of nature has been preserved and made accessible through the creation of national parks, forests, and monuments. Totaling over twenty-two million acres, these recreational spots are visited by more than forty-six million people annually. Yellowstone National Park, created in 1872 by the federal government, contains more than two million acres in the northwest corner of Wyoming and small slices of Montana and Idaho. In addition to magnificent scenery, it contains a large number of geysers, hot springs, mud volcanoes, waterfalls, lakes, and dense forests that provide refuge for deer, bear, elk, antelope, and other wild animals, which, protected by law from hunters, roam throughout the park. Here a few of the thirteen hundred thousand annual visitors to Yellowstone National Park watch "Old Faithful," a geyser that unfailingly erupts every hour, shooting a column of boiling water and steam 170 feet into the air. Primitive Indians believed that this weird land of ghostly mists, moaning mud volcanoes, and frightening eruptions was the abode of evil spirits and carefully avoided going near it.

Photo: National Park Service

Snow Provides Much Needed Water

An astute foreign observer once remarked that agrarian discontent in the United States is most intense west of the twenty-inch rainfall line. True or not, this remark was simply another recognition of the tremendous significance the scarcity of water has on every aspect of life in the arid West. Although irrigation was used by Indians of the Southwest for centuries before Columbus and was practiced at Spanish missions in California and the Southwest, it was first utilized by English-speaking people in the settlements in Utah and at the gold-mining sites where water used for washing gold was diverted for irrigating crops. Throughout the West, one of the principal sources of irrigation water is melted snow which in the spring rushes down precipitous canyons to mountain valleys, across thirsty plains, and over coastal flats into the sea. To capture this swift-moving runoff and store it for systematic use during the growing season for the production of crops has been the objective of farmers and irrigation engineers for three quarters of a century.

Photo: by Brockman, National Park Service

Cantaloupe Plants Under "Hot Caps" on Irrigated Land

Dry, barren, but fertile valleys have been converted into luxuriant fruit and vegetable gardens by the magic of irrigation and specialized techniques designed to produce succulent products for early or out-of-season markets. Here, plastic paper caps over wire frames protect tender cantaloupe plants from insects and diseases and provide a sun-heated shelter from chilling breezes. As the young plants mature, the paper disintegrates and wire frames are retrieved for future use.

Photo: USDA by Sikes

Wheat in the West Helps Feed the World

Despite dire forebodings of anti-plow Indians, drought, grasshopper plagues, rust damage, insect infestation, fires, hot winds, hail, brutal winters, and related difficulties, the Great Plains has become the Breadbasket of the World. In the anxious days following World War II, when famine stalked the earth, only the prodigious production of the Great Plains prevented mass starvation. The area which during the pioneer period was known as the "Great American Desert" now produces annually over thirty billion pounds of wheat in addition to many other crops and livestock products. Although wheat is produced in all of the forty-eight states, more than half the United States production is in the six states of North Dakota, South Dakota, Nebraska, Kansas, Oklahoma and Texas. Kansas is the largest producer.

USDA Photograph by McManigal

A Copper Mine Typifies Mineral Wealth

Most early settlements in the West were mining camps. Production of copper, silver, lead, gold, zinc, tungsten, and coal continues to be a major industry. In Arizona, Utah, Montana, and Colorado, huge mineral deposits have been worked for years, but enough remains to supply the needs of many generations, if properly utilized. Buried deep in the ground in remote mountain recesses, these mineral riches escaped the eyes of early explorers or were not considered valuable. Arizona leads in copper production, but Butte, Montana, is said to be located on the world's richest hill of copper, and Bingham, Utah, pictured here, is on a "mountain of copper." The Bingham copper mine covers about nine hundred acres; the ore lies so close to the surface that it can be mined with a steam shovel. The exposed surface from bottom level to the top is over nineteen hundred feet. The mineral wealth of the West has brought about a large increase in industrialization of the area in recent years.

Photo: Salt Lake Chamber of Commerce

Oil Wells on Oklahoma's Capitol Grounds

The first oil well in the United States was drilled in Pennsylvania in 1859, but real expansion in production came with the discovery of oil in Oklahoma, which occurred as the demand for petroleum to lubricate and propel the new automobile industry was growing large. The search for new oil fields went on frantically and, when successful, "black gold" boom towns flourished in the raucous manner reminiscent of gold rush days. The pitifully poor sandy hills and plains of Oklahoma that had been set aside as a permanent home for the Cherokee Indians of Georgia were found to be oil-laden and netted the Indians many millions of dollars.

Extensive oil deposits have been found in Texas, Kansas, California, and many other states, as well as in the sea off the shores of the United States. Transportation of oil to eager markets is accomplished by trucks, railroad tank cars, barges, ships, and by underground pipelines snaking their way across hundreds of miles.

Photo: Oklahoma Planning and Resources Board

"Football's Finest Hour"—The East-West Game

An adaptation of English rugby, American football lacked uniform rules and was frowned upon as brutal until Teddy Roosevelt, while President, called a conference, from which improvements resulted that eventually made football one of our greatest spectator sports. From September to December, high-school, college, and professional football teams dominate the sports pages, and on New Year's Day great crowds gather in stadiums around the country to watch the play of outstanding teams. In San Francisco, star athletes from the East compete with those from the West for the benefit of Shrine crippled children's hospitals in a game in which "strong legs run so that weak legs can walk." Over the years this game, which has been called "Football's Finest Hour," has raised over a million dollars to aid crippled children. Shown here is a crowd of sixty thousand people watching an East-West game in Kezar Stadium.

All forms of sport receive enthusiastic support in the United States, including baseball, basketball, boxing, and horse racing. Altogether, more than one-half billion admissions are paid annually by spectators at sports events.

Photo: San Francisco Chamber of Commerce

Chinatown in San Francisco

When gold was discovered near Sutter's Fort in 1848, San Francisco was a village nestling on the hilly shores of the world's largest landlocked harbor. Within a year, the little town had been transformed into a bustling port of more than twenty thousand population. As the West developed, so did San Francisco. Practically destroyed by the great earthquake and fire of 1906, San Francisco was rebuilt and has continued to grow, ranking eleventh among United States cities in 1950 with a population of 775,000, of whom 16,000 were of Chinese ancestry. More than a square mile of the city is occupied by Chinatown, the largest such area outside the Orient.

Photo: San Francisco Chamber of Commerce

A Wild Burro of the Desert

Burros long served as beasts of burden in mines, along treacherous mountain trails and in desert wastelands. Now displaced by machines many burros roam desert areas where they have acquired the alert cunning and wariness of wild animals.

Photo: U.S. Fish and Wildlife Service

Large Freight Trucks are Important in Transportation

Transportation still remains a major American problem despite modern facilities. Developments going back to colonial days include heavy-duty freight wagons like the Conestoga; river barges and keel boats; canals with mule-drawn barges; clipper ships; steamboats; farm wagons; the Red River cart; the Concord stagecoach; the covered wagon; railroads; automobiles; motor trucks; and finally the airplane.

The freight truck has revolutionized marketing and distribution methods during the past generation. With a vast network of good roads linking towns, cities, and rural areas, the motor truck can go practically anywhere at any time to pick up or deliver freight of almost any kind. This flexibility has resulted in trucks and trailers handling a large part of short-haul freight and has made them a major factor in long-distance movement of household goods, perishable fruits and vegetables, livestock, automobiles, and relatively lightweight manufactured articles.

About 98 per cent of America's eggs are moved from farm to market by truck, 85 per cent of poultry, 80 per cent of livestock, and 50 per cent of fruit and vegetables.

Photo: American Trucking Association

The Search for Uranium

About the time the dinosaur, whose preserved frame can be seen in the National Museum, passed away some hundred and twenty-five million years ago in the marshes of Utah and Colorado, uranium-bearing sands were laid down over the area. Time rolled by—eons of time—and finally Indians found a use for the red, yellow, and green uranium minerals as war paint. Later, radium was extracted from the ore and used in medical research, especially by Pierre and Madame Curie. After World War I vanadium also was taken from the ore and used in the production of steel. Then came World War II and the need for tremendous quantities of uranium for use in the atomic bomb. Peacetime development of atomic energy for industrial uses caused a scramble to discover new deposits of uranium reminiscent of gold rush days. However, the plodding prospector wandering over the wasteland in his lonesome search for riches gave way to highly skilled workmen using scientific methods. The Geiger counter, bulldozers, heavy trucks, airplanes, and thousands of competent, trained workers in a joint effort of government and private enterprise quickly made the high plateau the principal source of uranium in the United States. In Colorado, Utah, Arizona, and New Mexico large areas long considered of little productive value turned out to be a treasureland in the atomic age.

Photo: Union Carbide and Carbon Corporation

Birthplace of a President

The maturing of the West is indicated by the fact that the United States elected in 1952 the first President to be born west of the Missouri River. Eisenhower, like Washington, Jefferson, Jackson, Lincoln, and most of the other thirty-two Presidents, was born amidst modest circumstances and made his way to the White House through his own energy, ability, and character. Such a career is assurance that 464 years after Columbus discovered the New World and 180 years after the founding of the new republic, the American people still cherish the principles of freedom of opportunity and the "aristocracy of talents" which were among the foundation stones of the nation. Shortly after the Civil War a young minister named Horatio Alger, working with poor boys in New York City, started writing books based on the lives of boys he saw around him. In the Alger books the hero invariably was a poor but brave, honest, intelligent boy who gained fame and fortune through his own endeavors. Happily for America, such dreams can still come true.

Photo: Kansas Department of Commerce and Industry

A Preacher from the Hills

This review of the story of the U.S.A. ends where it began—with people of character, faith, and courage. Here, the Reverend J. B. Gragg, "a preacher from the hills," prays for the people of the world to put away evil and live in peace.

The chapters in tomorrow's story of this country are obscure and can be indicated only by the happenings of yesterday. As Patrick Henry put it, "I know of no way of judging the future but by the past."

North Carolina Department of Conservation and Development

BIBLIOGRAPHY
OF SELECTED REFERENCES

ADAMS, JAMES TRUSLOW. *The Epic of America*. New York: Cornwall Press, 1931.

ANDERSON, RUDOLPH E. *The Story of the American Automobile*. Washington, D.C.: Public Affairs Press, 1950.

ANDREWS, MATHEW PAGE. *History of Maryland*. New York: Doubleday, 1929.

BILLINGTON, RAY ALLEN, AND J. B. HEDGES. *Westward Expansion*. New York: Macmillan, 1949.

BOTKIN, B. A. (ed.) *A Treasury of American Folklore*. New York: Crown, 1944.

BOWERS, CLAUDE G. *The Tragic Era*. Toronto: McClelland & Stewart, 1937.

BOWERS, CLAUDE G. *Hamilton and Jefferson*. Boston: Houghton Mifflin, 1945.

CLARK, ARTHUR H. *The Clipper Ship Era*. New York: Putnam, 1910.

COY, HAROLD. *George Washington Carver*. New.York: Doubleday, 1951.

CRAVEN, WESLEY FRANK. *Southern Colonies in the Seventeenth Century*. Baton Rouge: Louisiana State University Press, 1949.

FOWLER, HARLAN D. *Camels to California*. Stanford: Stanford University Press, 1951.

GRAHAM, PHILIP. *Showboats*. Austin: University of Texas Press, 1951.

HAWK, EMORY QUINTER. *Economic History of the South*. New York: Prentice-Hall, 1934.

HICKS, JOHN D. *Federal Union*. Boston: Houghton Mifflin, 1948.

HINCKLEY, GORDON B. *What of the Mormons?* Salt Lake City: Deseret Book Company, 1950.

HUNTER, J. MARVIN, AND NOAH H. ROSE. *Album of Gun Fighters*. Bandera, Texas: J. M. Hunter, 1951.

IRVING, WASHINGTON. *Astoria and Anecdotes of an Enterprise*. Portland, Ore.: Binfords and Mort, 1950.

KANE, HARNETT T. *Natchez on the Mississippi*. New York: Morrow, 1947.

MACE, WM. H., AND FRANK S. BOGARDUS. *History of the United States*. Chicago: Rand McNally, 1926.

NATIONAL LIVESTOCK HISTORICAL ASS'N. *Prose and Poetry of the Livestock Industry*. Chicago: Franklin Hudson, 1905.

OLMSTED, FREDERICK LAW. *The Cotton Kingdom*. New York: Knopf, 1953.

OWESLEY, FRANK LAWRENCE. *State Rights in the Confederacy*. Chicago: University of Chicago Press, 1925.

PAULLIN, CHARLES O. *Atlas of the Historical Geography of the U. S.* Carnegie Institution of Washington and American Geographical Society of New York, 1932.

PELZER, LOUIS. *Marches of the Dragoons in the Mississippi Valley*. Iowa City: State Historical Society of Iowa, 1917.

RAINE, WILLIAM MACLEOD. *Famous Sheriffs and Western Outlaws*. New York: New Home Library, 1929.

ROOSEVELT, THEODORE. *The Winning of the West*. New York: Review of Reviews, 1904.

SCHMIDT, LOUIS BERNARD, AND EARLE DUDLEY ROSS. *Readings of the Economic History of Agriculture*. New York: Macmillan, 1925.

SHURTLEFF, HAROLD. *The Log Cabin Myth*. Cambridge: Harvard University Press, 1939.

SMITH, ALFRED E. *Up to Now*. New York: Viking, 1929.

SMITH, J. FRAZIER. *White Pillars—The Architecture of the South*. New York: William Helburn, 1941.

SMITH, J. RUSSELL. *North America*. New York: Harcourt, Brace, 1925.

TURNER, FREDERICK JACKSON. *The Frontier in American History*. Gloucester, Mass.: Peter Smith, 1950.

VERRILL, A. HYATT. *Great Conquerors of South and Central America*. New York: New Home Library, 1943.

WASHINGTON, BOOKER T. *Up From Slavery*. New York: Oxford University Press, 1945.

WEBB, WALTER PRESCOTT. *The Great Plains*. Boston: Ginn, 1931.

WERTENBAKER, THOMAS JEFFERSON. *The First Americans—1607–1690*. New York: Macmillan, 1927.

WILGUS, A. CURTIS. *The Development of Hispanic America*. New York: Farrar and Rinehart, 1941.

WILLIAMS, JAMES MICKEL. *The Expansion of Rural Life*. New York: Crofts, 1926.

WOODWARD, C. V. *Origins of the New South*. Baton Rouge: Louisiana State University Press, 1951.

Miscellaneous References:

The Story of the American Patent System. Washington, D.C.: Patent Office, 1940.

Historical Statistics of the U.S.—1879–1945. Washington, D.C.: Department of Agriculture, 1949.

A Supplement to the Statistical Abstract. Washington, D.C.: Bureau of the Census, 1949.

American Guide Series, Writer's Project

New Mexico. New York: Hastings House, 1940.

Missouri. New York: Duell, Sloan & Pearce, 1941.

Index